McKinley and DeMars are  are also two of the most fa. know. So when I heard they were getting together to write a short book on the Prosperity Gospel, I got excited. I've read the book now, and I was right to be excited! It is insightful and humorous, wise and winsome, direct yet careful. I pray that God will cause your soul to prosper as you read this book.

Mark Dever
Senior Pastor, Capitol Hill Baptist Church and President,
9Marks.org, Washington, DC

Sean and Michael have written an honest and illuminating book that uses scripture (in context!) to confront all the core tenets of the prosperity gospel. If you have a loved one caught in this deception, this book will be a useful evangelistic tool to unravel the man-centered twisting of the good news. The heart behind this book comes from the personal experience of the authors who have witnessed, first-hand, the damage that this poisonous doctrine can inflict on one's faith in Christ. It is also written in a way that is conversational, speaking the truth with directness in love. I pray the Lord will use this work to graciously reveal the glory of the true Christ to those in deception.

Brandon Kimber
Director of 'American Gospel: Christ Alone'

Invented in the United States of America, the Prosperity Gospel has now become the face of Christianity around much of the world. It is truly our worst export. I am so grateful for this book by Sean DeMars and Michael Mckinley.

It is a very readable and a thoroughly biblical exposure .... I commend this book to you and encourage you to share it with friends and family members who are trapped in the prosperity deception.

Justin Peters
Founder of Justin Peters Ministries

THE PROSPERITY GOSPEL MEETS THE TRUTHS OF SCRIPTURE

HEALTH

WEALTH

AND THE

(REAL) GOSPEL

SEAN DEMARS AND MIKE MCKINLEY

Copyright © Sean DeMars and Mike McKinley 2022

Paperback ISBN: 978-1-5271-0802-8
Ebook ISBN: 978-1-5271-0880-6

Published in 2022
by
Christian Focus Publications Ltd,
Geanies House, Fearn, Ross-shire
IV20 1TW, Scotland
www.christianfocus.com

Cover design by James Amour

Printed and bound by
Bell & Bain, Glasgow

CONTENTS

Introduction – Would Jesus Hate this Book?

Sean here. I'm a pastor in Alabama, and I'm a survivor of the prosperity gospel. Here's the brief version of my story: I didn't grow up in the church. As a kid, while most of my Christian friends were hustling memory verses for jewels in their Awana crowns, I was watching Eddie Murphy's *Delirious* for the 900th time. When the Lord saved me from my sins at the age of eighteen, I had a lot of catching up to do. Moses, Abraham, Samson, Elihu…I'd never heard of 'em. And maybe it wouldn't have been that hard to catch up had I been warmly received into a good, gospel-preaching, Bible-believing church. But I didn't seem to really fit in at any of those churches, and I didn't stick around long enough to learn the things I needed to know.

You see, just a few months before being saved, I was walking around with a gun in my pants. Or under the seat of my car. Or under my pillow at night. As a drug dealer, I needed a weapon close at hand at all times.

As you might imagine, drug dealers have a certain image they need to maintain. They have to look the part, and I most certainly did. I wore an A-frame tank top (also known as a 'wife-beater' by those in my neck of the woods), sagging shorts, a cut in my eyebrow, a bandana in my back pocket, and about as much physical aggression as I could exude at any moment in time.

When I got saved out of that lifestyle, my heart may have changed, but my wardrobe largely remained the same. I was still extremely aggressive, but now I was aggressive for Jesus. I was a poor man's Nicky Cruz (*The Cross and the Switchblade* guy). Youth pastors from all over the great expanse of North Alabama invited me to come and share my testimony with their students—and the more war stories, the better. Many of these churches were happy to have me put on a 'scared straight' clinic for their teenagers, but they didn't seem too keen on keeping me around after the lights came on in the youth room. And who could blame them? I still had a gold grill with vampire teeth at the bottom. Scary stuff.

What this meant for my discipleship, however, was that there wasn't any. Which is tragic, because I desperately needed help. Do you remember how Paul talks about zeal without knowledge (Rom. 10:1-3)? Well, that was me. I was evangelizing anyone who would listen, and even some who wouldn't. One of my major plans for evangelism involved me climbing onto the roof of a fast food establishment and preaching the gospel to the drive-thru customers. But I really had no idea what I was doing. The only thing I knew was that Jesus had saved me, and I wanted other people to be saved, too. I wanted to be Christ's ambassador, as if the Lord

Jesus were making His appeal through me, 'Be reconciled to God!' (2 Cor. 5:20)

Just a few months into stumbling along the path of righteousness with no real guide, a man in my neighborhood saw me walking around with a Bible in my hand. This man invited me into his home, bought me lunch, and then finally got around to asking me if I understood what was really going on in that book I was carrying. I assured him that I understood most of it…maybe. Truthfully, however, the Bible was like a German refrigerator manual to me.

I don't speak German. Nor do I know anything about refrigerators.

Over the next twelve to fifteen months, this man discipled me in God's Word. Or so I thought. As a new Christian, my doctrinal discernment was at what physicists and theologians alike describe as 'absolute zero.' Let me give you an example. I still remember calling someone an idiot during Bible study for saying that Jesus was a Jew. 'How can this guy not know that Jesus was a CHRISTIAN?!' I muttered under my breath. If you don't know, that's OK, but let me tell you that Jesus was totally a Jew.

So when someone told me that sickness is the result of either sin or lack of faith, I didn't know any better. When I was told that going to the doctor was a sin—because illness is a spiritual condition, not a physical one—I almost died of mercury poisoning. When someone used the Bible to convince me that we were supposed to rebuke poverty with the power of our speech, I started calling out my (sometimes negative) ATM balance.

It wasn't until later that I could see that these teachings were a combination of silly, dangerous, and spiritually toxic. What this man taught me wasn't the gospel at all, but a distortion of it. At the time, I couldn't see that this 'prosperity gospel' wasn't good news. I had no idea it was an untrue message that couldn't save anyone. Now I realize that what we believe about things like faith, the cross, physical healing, and spiritual victory really matters. When we misunderstand and distort the gospel, people get hurt—in this life and even eternally.

***

Mike here. I'm a pastor in Virginia. I never sold drugs or rebuked my (sometimes negative) ATM balance. And once my family started going to church, we went to a solid church that preached the Bible clearly. But I've still had my fair share of run-ins with the prosperity gospel. As a pastor, I've seen people's suffering made worse by a sense that they were somehow responsible, that their circumstances were a result of a failure of their faith or holiness. I've seen others seduced away from the faith by promises of material blessings and long life.

The danger of the prosperity gospel hit home for me when my lovely wife, Karen, was diagnosed with Multiple Sclerosis in 2006. As you can imagine, it was an upsetting, confusing, and even frightening experience for us. We couldn't help but wonder why this was happening, what it meant for our future, and how we would manage if Karen became really ill. It was the kind of situation that drives you to your church family for support and strength. And sure enough, lots of Christians said very helpful things to her about God's love and power and His good plans for her life. We were strengthened and encouraged by these brothers and sisters.

At the same time, some Christians said silly things about the dangers of drinking out of plastic bottles and the curative power of certain herbs. We rolled our eyes a bit and tried to take these comments with good humor. But a few Christians we knew said some really unhelpful things to her about faith and healing—that it couldn't possibly be God's will for her to be sick and that she would rebuke her illness if she had enough faith. This was the prosperity gospel, and it was maddening to me. Karen was one of the most faithful and sacrificial followers of Jesus that I know. That last thing she needed in her suffering was to have false guilt and unnecessary blame heaped on her.

My interest in this book comes from seeing all of the people who are hurt and misled by false teaching. I've been in India and Africa, where prosperity gospel preachers attract many thousands of people with their promises of riches, health, and blessings—never mind the fact that their promises never come to pass! I've seen the pain and frustration on the faces of faithful pastors in those places when false teachers come along and lead their sheep astray. I want to help you to understand what the prosperity gospel is, why it is so dangerous, and why the real good news is so much better.

***

We're writing this book for two audiences. First, we're writing it for you if you belong to a faithful gospel-preaching church, but you have friends or family members in a prosperity church. Or you wonder if they're in such a church. You've heard them talk about their preacher's sermons. You can tell something is wrong. But you can't quite put your finger on it. Plus, they have plenty of Bible verses to back up their claims. You love them and are worried about them. Our goal is to help you put your finger on exactly what's wrong.

Second, we're writing it for you if you yourself belong or suspect you belong to a prosperity gospel church. We want to help you to ask good questions about what your church teaches. No, we're not trying to cultivate a crowd of critics, but we do want to make sure you understand what is and what is not the gospel. It's the most important piece of news you'll ever know, both for your sake and for the sake of those you love. So you want to make sure you get it right!

Even the apostle Paul said to the members of the Galatian churches, he didn't care if someone showed up their churches and flashed the apostle card or if an angel flew down from heaven on wings: if that person taught a false gospel, it was up to the members of those churches to kick that false teacher out (see Gal. 1:6-9). By that token, both of us will tell the members of our church to fire us (!) if we ever teach a false gospel.

Still, maybe you wonder, why would we attack ministers who seem to be turning millions of people to Jesus? Even if we have some concerns about the content of their teachings, shouldn't we applaud the fact that the Bible is being preached and Jesus is being lifted up? Sure, they may get some things wrong, but isn't it worse to be a negative and critical person? After all, didn't Jesus tell us not to judge (Matt. 7:1)? And didn't He say that whoever is not against us is for us (Mark 9:40)? In short, would Jesus hate this book?

We don't think so. Yes, of course He taught us not to be judgmental people (which is the point of Matthew 7:1). But everyone exercises judgment when they decide which doctor to see or which restaurant to frequent. If you saw that a surgeon had his license suspended repeatedly, you would (wisely) judge that he is not someone you should trust with your health. If you saw that a restaurant was shut down for health code violations, you would (correctly) judge that you should find another place to eat.

Prosperity gospel teachers are more dangerous than an inept surgeon or a roach-infested restaurant. Those things might make you ill; they might even shorten your life. But if you believe false things about Jesus, if you don't understand what it means to be saved by Him or to be His disciple, the consequences are disastrous for eternity.

In many cases, it's wise to give people the benefit of the doubt. The love that the Holy Spirit produces in us leads us to believe the best about others. It's quite possible that many prosperity gospel preachers sincerely believe what they are teaching; they think they're helping people. So if you're uncomfortable by a book devoted to criticizing and challenging these preachers, we get it.

But consider: Jesus repeatedly warned us about the prosperity gospel. He didn't think it was something to be embraced or even tolerated. He attacked it in the sharpest terms because He loves us and wants to vaccinate us against this deadly spiritual disease.

Nowhere do we see this more clearly than in Jesus' words near the end of the Sermon on the Mount. So let's look at two matters that Jesus addressed in Matthew 7, not too long after He warned us not to be judgmental. First, Jesus says:

> Enter by the narrow gate. For the gate is wide and the way is easy that leads to destruction, and those who enter by it are many. For the gate is narrow and the way is hard that leads to life, and those who find it are few. (Matt. 7:13-14)

Jesus' point is clear: the way that leads to life is difficult. In context, it seems that this difficult way is the one He'd been laying out earlier in the Sermon on the Mount. It's the way of forgiving your enemies (Matt. 5:44), mourning your sin (Matt. 5:4), and thirsting for righteousness (Matt. 5:6). It's the way of marital faithfulness and sexual purity (Matt. 5:27-30), of meekness and humility (Matt. 5:5), of truth-telling (Matt. 5:37). It's the way of turning the other cheek (Matt. 5:39) and going the extra mile (Matt. 5:41). None of those matters are easy and pleasant. As a result, this path isn't crowded with travelers.

In contrast, it's very easy to wander down the road that leads to spiritual destruction. This is the path for the disinterested, the hypocritical, and the deceived. It's the path for people who want to live any way they want to live, to avoid difficulty and sacrifice and self-denial. If you want to do whatever seems right to you, if you need to have ease and pleasure now, then the easy path is the one for you.

Much of what Jesus teaches in the Sermon on the Mount boils down to the value of delayed gratification. If you want your best life now, then take the easy path. It won't be so great for you in the end, but it'll 'feel good' for a little while. The Beatitudes (Matt. 5:3-11), on the other hand, teach us that if you want someday to be comforted, if you want to see God, if you want to inherit the earth, if you want to be satisfied in the end, if you want a great reward in heaven, then it's going to be difficult now.

Maybe you can begin to see how this applies to the prosperity gospel. But we're not finished yet. Look at what Jesus says next: 'Beware of false prophets, who come to you in sheep's clothing but inwardly are ravenous wolves' (Matt. 7:15).

It's hard to overstate what Jesus says here. After warning us about the destruction that results from taking the easy path, He immediately alerts us to the danger posed by false prophets. A false prophet is someone who leads people onto the wrong path. A false prophet calls his victims to walk the easy road that leads to destruction; he assures them that they can have it all—in both this life and the next.

Picture those two gates and paths in your mind. Now imagine that outside the gates are two tour guides. Both have maps of their respective paths, both claim that theirs is the way that leads to life, and both tell you that listening to the other guy is going to cost you dearly. According to Jesus, it matters quite a bit which tour guide you choose. If you allow yourself to be convinced to head down the wrong path, the consequences will be terrible.

And so Jesus instructs us to 'beware.' He wants us to be attentive, to be picky, and to pay attention to what we hear and whom we follow. Because false teachers don't normally come to us with their claws out, drooling and baring their fangs. Instead, they look just like another sheep. That's how they gain entrance into the flock, lull the sheep into a false sense of security, and finally prey on their victims.

False teachers don't come to us saying, 'Just to be clear, I am a false prophet. If you listen to me, your soul will be endangered. I will now propose that you participate in rank evil.' If they did, no one would be deceived! Instead, false teachers come with a mixture of truth, speculation, and innovation. What they say *makes sense*, but only if you ignore other biblical truths. They might teach something you *wish* Jesus had taught, even if you're pretty sure He didn't. We have to watch out for teachers who seem like one of the sheep, but who actually are tour guides on a path that leads to hell.

If prosperity gospel teachers aren't teaching what Jesus taught, then we absolutely cannot afford to coddle them or tolerate their message. In the end, you should judge everything you hear and read (including this book!) by the truths of Scripture. We intend to make the case that the prosperity gospel is a dangerous lie that must be exposed and resisted. So let's get to it.

1. The Heart of the Prosperity Gospel

It seems like our first order of business should be to define our terms. We need to establish what we mean by the 'prosperity gospel' (from this point on, we are going to refer to it as 'PG'—the trees in the rain forest can thank us later). This task of definition is more complicated than it seems. After all, there aren't any universally recognized creeds or authoritative central governing bodies among the churches, preachers, and media outlets that make up the PG world.

Maybe it's easiest to see the PG as something like water. Water is always two hydrogen atoms and one oxygen atom bonded together. But it can look different under different conditions. Whether ice, steam, or liquid, water is always water.

Similarly, there are many different manifestations of the PG. But they all share the same basic elements. We'll list four of the most prominent.

1. Prosperity Gospel: God Wants to Bless You Materially!

The Problem: It Puts Our Focus on the Gift More than the Giver.

Think about the last time you gave a gift to someone you really care about. Maybe it was a Christmas present for a friend, an anniversary gift for your spouse, or a birthday present for your child. Whatever the circumstances, it's likely that you intended that gift to be an expression of your care and love for that person.

A few years ago, my (Mike's) wife made me a blanket out of a bunch of my favorite old band T-shirts. Every time I see the blanket in my office, I'm reminded of how much time and care and effort went into making that gift. I really treasure the gift—not just because it's the perfect size and weight for a blanket, but because Karen made it for me as an expression of her love.

What if I loved the blanket but never connected it back to Karen in my heart? What if I enjoyed the gift whenever I was reading a book and my office was a bit chilly, but I never thought of her and her kindness and love? Would you think that the purpose of the gift had been fully achieved? On one level, the blanket keeps me warm, so there's that. But it was meant to do more than that; it was meant to remind me of my wife's love.

It's the same way with the gifts God gives us. When the apostle Paul was speaking to the people of Athens, he told them that God 'gives to all mankind life and breath and everything' for a reason. 'That they should seek God, and perhaps feel their way toward him and find him' (Acts 17:25b, 27a). In short, God's gifts are meant to lead our thoughts and our hearts back to Him the way that a stream leads back to its spring.

It's fair to say that the PG strongly emphasizes receiving, maintaining, and even maximizing the good gifts of God (health, wealth, favor, power). And yet, there's relatively little emphasis on God Himself. Now, we want to be fair—no PG preacher that we know of would nakedly state that people ought to love God's gifts *more* than they love God. And if you asked them, they would surely deny that this is what they teach. But we're talking about emphasis and priority. When you see a church or ministry that talks about God's gifts but spends relatively little time talking about God's character or our need to respond to Him in repentance and faith, then you can be pretty sure you're dealing with the PG.

Here's one example from the ministry of Benny Hinn. He writes:

> We have many instances of the wealth transfer in Bible history, including Israel's. Remember the great Old Testament superpower called Egypt? The nation had more gold and silver than any other on the planet. Yet Moses was in exile in the desert while the children of Israel toiled in slavery. Everything kept going as it had been for years, but suddenly things began to change. God spoke to Moses from a burning bush and told him to go back to Egypt. Not only

did He promise to deliver His children from slavery, but He said, 'When you leave you will not go empty-handed.'[1]

It's not that what Hinn is saying is false, but he puts the emphasis in all the wrong places. Yes, the Lord blessed the people of Israel materially as they left Egypt, but that's hardly the point of the story. God's people got a lot more out of the deal than some gold and jewels. The headline isn't 'God Transfers Wealth From Egypt to Israel' but 'God Keeps His Promise and Powerfully Delivers His People From Their Enemies.' Over and over again, the Bible points to Israel's deliverance from slavery as the Old Testament's clearest picture of God's salvation. The exodus event was a shadow of the coming deliverance that Christ would bring (see Exod. 20:1, Isa. 11:16, Luke 9:30-31). In the exodus, God's power and love are on full display, and it ought to make His people worship Him. To reduce these events to little more than a transfer of wealth is to miss the point. It's to value the gift over the giver.

If you want to see what it looks like to get the whole 'gift-giver' thing right, look no further than Asaph in Psalm 73. After confessing that he was tempted to be envious of the ways that other people prospered (particularly the wicked), he concluded:

Whom have I in heaven but you?
  And there is nothing on earth that I desire besides you.
My flesh and my heart may fail,

---

1   https://www.bennyhinn.org/enewsletter/greatest-wealth-transfer/ Accessed October 12, 2019.

but God is the strength of my heart and
my portion forever. (Ps. 73:25-26)

Asaph wrestles through the suffering of the righteous and the prosperity of the wicked, but finally consoles himself with the reality that ultimately his greatest treasure is not God's gifts, but God Himself. The psalmist has found something that resolves his frustrations and alleviates his suffering: he has found true joy and pleasure in God.

In the PG, however, God is spoken of primarily as a means to an end. It treats a relationship with God like marrying someone for their money. You don't really love them; you just love them for what they can give you. But coming to Jesus as a way to get something else isn't worship, it's idolatry of the thing you're trying to get.

If you're in a church and you're wondering whether or not they're influenced by the PG, simply pay attention to the sermons, the Bible study during group discussions, and the prayer meetings throughout the week. If your pastor—or Sunday school teacher, favorite author, et. al.—spends a small amount of time talking about what God is like, but a lot of time talking about what God can give you, then you're probably face-to-face with the PG.

2. Prosperity Gospel: God Wants Us to Speak with Power

The Problem: It Confuses Creatures and Their Creator.

One of the most fundamental truths of Scripture is that God is our creator and we are His creatures. This seems like a fairly obvious reality. And yet, over and over God sees the need to clarify: He's not like us, and we aren't exactly like Him. Here's a very brief sampling of ways that we are not like God:

- God made everything that exists out of nothing (Heb. 11:3, Rev. 4:11). We can make things (hooray for art and creativity!), but we cannot create *anything* out of nothing.
- God doesn't have any needs (Psalm 50:8-15, Isaiah 40:14, Acts 17:24-25). We, however, are dependent and cannot survive unless God provides for us (Matt. 6:11).
- God doesn't have a beginning (Isa. 57:15, Rev. 1:8). We, obviously, do.
- God can do anything He wants to do (Dan. 4:34-35, Ps. 115:3). Our power and abilities are limited.
- God knows everything and He's never wrong (Rom. 11:33, Ps. 147:5). We know some things, but definitely not everything. We are often wrong.

Since people are made in God's image, we are capable of reflecting many of God's qualities (love, wisdom, strength, holiness). But we shouldn't lose sight of the fact that God is infinitely more loving, wiser, stronger, and holier than we are.

> For as the heavens are higher than the earth,
>> so are my ways higher than your ways
>> and my thoughts than your thoughts. (Isa. 55:9)

PG teachers tend to obscure this distinction between God and us. They encourage their followers to believe that they can do things that only God can do. They may recognize that God works on a different scale and with greater power, but they distort the Scriptures and encourage human beings to act like God and think too highly of themselves.

Here's an example from Kenneth Copeland's ministry:

> Like it or not, this is a word-created, word-controlled universe. God established it that way from the very beginning. He made everything by calling 'things which be not as though they were' (Romans 4:17, KJV). He set this whole system in motion by speaking into the darkness and saying, 'Light be!' and light was. (Gen. 1:3)

> The whole Bible, from Genesis to Revelation, makes it clear that we live under a word-activated system. It's always been that way, and it always will be. We can't change that fact. We can, however, choose the words under which we live. We can change our environment by what we say....

> *God has delegated authority here on earth to you.* Your words have authority to create every time you speak, not just when you pray. If you speak positive results in prayer and negative results the rest of the time, your negative words will prevail....

> Speak whatever you desire to come to pass in the Name of Jesus. Take authority over the money you need, and command it to come to you. If you need healing, speak to your body. Command it to be healed in the Name of Jesus. Command it to function properly. Speak the result you want. Whatever you say will come to pass.[2]

---

2   https://blog.kcm.org/words-start-button-everything-youre-believing/
     accessed October 15, 2019, italics ours

Can you see the way that this kind of teaching blurs the lines between the creature and the creator? Again, some of what he says is *true*. God did create the world out of nothing with His powerful, creative speech. And our speech does have the power to do great harm or great good (James 3:1-12). But nothing in the Bible encourages us to think that our speech has the power to accomplish whatever we want; that power belongs to God alone. Despite what Copeland says, the Bible decidedly does *not* teach that God has delegated this kind of power and authority to us.

You might be thinking, 'Wait a minute! What about Proverbs 18:21? Doesn't the Bible tells us that "death and life are in the power of the tongue"?' PG preachers love this verse; they love to quote it as proof that we can bring our desires to pass with our speech. But is that what that passage really means? Absolutely not.

When I (Sean) was deep in the prosperity gospel, I was told to rebuke my ATM receipt when it said that I was forty dollars overdrawn. I was told that if I said the right words in perfect faith, then reality would bend to my wishes. So I went for it: 'I rebuke this account balance, and Satan's overdraft fees to boot!' Despite all my faith and belief, not once could I make money appear in my bank account.

Proverbs 18:21 is definitely true, and Kenneth Copeland is definitely wrong. This passage is similar to James 3 in that it teaches us about the impact our words have on others, for good or for ill. It has nothing to do with our words' creative or destructive powers in a literal sense. God alone has the power to give life and take life because He is the only creator and sustainer of the world. 'See now that I, even I, am he, and there is no god beside me; I kill and I make alive; I wound and I heal; and there is none that can deliver out of my hand' (Deut. 32:39).

Some PG preachers will point to Jesus' life and ministry as our example in this. But that's wrong, too, for the simple reason that we're not God. God the Father has granted unique authority to the Lord Jesus Christ because, as God the Son, He is a unique person (Matt. 11:27, Matt. 28:18). That is why, through the power of the Holy Spirit, Jesus could perform miracles, cast out demons, and raise the dead. On two occasions, Jesus conferred some of His authority on His disciples for a fixed missionary task (Matt. 10:1, Luke 10:19). And it's true that the book of Acts depicts apostles performing signs and wonders (including raising the dead). But nowhere in the New Testament are we led to believe that this kind of power and authority is available to anyone who speaks their words in faith.

3. Prosperity Gospel: God Doesn't Want Us to Suffer!

The Problem: God Promises His People Will Suffer in the World.

I (Sean) remember sitting in church one Sunday morning, listening to the pastor preach. He was a sight to behold, with his perfect smile and seemingly tailored leather jacket. He had helicoptered in from the church's other campus just to be with us in person. We felt so lucky to have this blessed man of God with us! The sermon that morning was about one thing and one thing only: God's hatred of suffering. I still remember the way he drove the point home, 'God is our father, and no father wants to see his children suffer. Earthly fathers can't stop their children from suffering, but our Father in heaven can.'

The logic of the sermon went like this: God won't *allow* us to suffer. So if we *do* suffer, it's because we haven't been walking in the will of the Lord. If our lives are difficult, the cause is clear. It must be some kind of sin or lack of faith in God's promises. As I sat there and listened, the whole system seemed to make sense.

This kind of thinking pervades the PG. Bill Johnson, the leader of the Bethel Church movement, once answered the question 'Is it always God's will to heal someone?' on his personal website. After saying *yes*, he then advised those who were seeking to perform miraculous healings. If they fail, he said, we must remember that 'there are no deficiencies on His end—neither the covenant is deficient, nor His compassion or promises. All lack is on our end of the equation…. If someone isn't healed, realize the problem isn't God, and seek Him for direction as well as personal breakthrough (greater anointing for consistency in healing).'

In his story of how he left the PG, Costi Hinn (Benny Hinn's nephew and sometimes ministry associate) wrote about the time his mother's cancer diagnosis shook his confidence in his family's theology of illness. He reflects:

> The Hinn family never got sick. Or at least we never admitted it when we were. Sickness that was supposed to stay so far from our home had infiltrated the heartbeat of our home—

my mum…. During that time, my father downplayed her sickness. He preached that we were all to be healthy and whole while my own mother sat silently in the front row with a tumor waging war on her brain. Doctor's visits were done when my father was out of town. My mother hid her negative reports, and if she even hinted at the word tumor, my father would rebuke her and the word tumor in the name of Jesus. Finally, however, all the prosperity gospel power in the world could do nothing. With no choice but to pursue medical intervention, they faced the facts. It would be a surgeon's hand that healed my mother.[3]

This kind of thinking is deadly. It denies the reality that God works through doctors and medicine to heal us. But that's not all: the PG also heaps loads of guilt, shame, and fear on suffering people.

Oh, and it also seems to completely ignore the Bible's witness on the topic of suffering.

All throughout the Bible, God's people suffer. Sometimes their suffering is the result of their sin (e.g., 2 Sam. 12:19, Ps. 32:3-4). But we also see in Scripture that painful circumstances come to innocent people because God has a more ultimate purpose than a person's comfort and health (e.g., Gen. 50:20, Job 1, John 9:1-3, 2 Cor. 12:7-10). This is certainly true of the sufferings of the perfectly innocent and faithful Lord Jesus, which were clearly the will of God (e.g., Isa. 53:10, Acts 4:27-28).

It's also clear that New Testament authors believed suffering would be a regular part of every Christian's

---

3   Costi Hinn, *God, Greed, and the (Prosperity) Gospel* (Grand Rapids, MI: Zondervan, 2019), p. 126.

experience—not just the 'heroes' of the faith. Consider the following verses:

> Blessed are you when others revile you and persecute you and utter all kinds of evil against you falsely on my account. Rejoice and be glad, for your reward is great in heaven, for so they persecuted the prophets who were before you. (Matt. 5:11-12)

> For it has been granted to you that for the sake of Christ you should not only believe in him but also suffer for his sake. (Phil. 1:29)

> Yet if anyone suffers as a Christian, let him not be ashamed, but let him glorify God in that name. (1 Pet. 4:16)

Unfortunately, PG teachers make Christians feel ashamed of their sufferings. They tell people that God *always* wills to heal *every* disease. They tell them their suffering is outside God's will.

The Bible's teaching is much more complex. Sometimes, God shows His love and power by healing and sparing His people from suffering. Other times, God does not spare His people from their pain and difficulty. On these occasions, He still brings Himself glory—whether He saves them from their sickness or not. Why does God decide to save Persons A, B, and C and not Persons X, Y, and Z? Who knows the mind of our God, and who can bring counsel to Him (Rom. 11:33)? In every case, He remains all-powerful and all-good.

We must feel the tension in this. Doing so proves we are reading Scripture rightly. The PG, on the other hand, seeks to alleviate this tension by flattening the Bible's portrayal of a difficult topic. In other words, its portrayal of suffering is both shallow and unbiblical. Where you find this, the PG probably isn't far behind.

4. Prosperity Gospel: God Wants Us to Live the Victorious, Prosperous Life!

The Problem: Scripture teaches the faithful Christian life can't be reduced to a few themes.

In her excellent book *Blessed*, Kate Bowler provides a history of the PG. She notes that the prosperity gospel tends to focus on four main themes:

1. Faith
2. Wealth
3. Health
4. Victory[4]

If every text of Scripture ends with teaching one of those four themes, then you're almost certainly in a PG church. You may also notice that many PG teachers consistently come back to the same, out-of-context verses and conveniently avoid passages of Scripture like the ones quoted above.

To be clear, there's nothing wrong with talking about faith, wealth, health, and victory. But it's also important to note that those aren't the only matters that the Bible talks about. A true minister of the gospel should be able to echo the apostle Paul, who declared himself innocent of

---

4   Kate Bowler, *Blessed: A History of the American Prosperity Gospel* (Oxford: Oxford University Press, 2013), p. 7.

his hearers' blood, for he did not shrink from declaring to them the whole counsel of God (Acts 20:26-27). God's flock needs to be fed from every part of God's Word. We need to know what God says about suffering as much as we need to know what He says about prosperity. God uses both to make us more like His Son, Jesus.

PG ministers use the words 'faith,' 'wealth,' 'health,' and 'victory' a lot. But they rarely mean what the Bible means. In fact, this is how PG ministers infuse their false teaching into the church. They use pious words, but they change their meaning. This is called 'twisting Scripture' (2 Pet. 3:16).

You might say that we're separated from the PG by a common language. Think about the ways people in different places use the English language. Australians call their schedules 'diaries.' The Brits call the trunk of a car the 'boot.' South Africans call traffic lights 'robots.' We're separated by a common language; we use many of the same words, but we don't always use them to mean the same things.

Now imagine that two professing Christians—one from a PG church, the other from an evangelical church—swap churches for a Sunday. They might both hear about faith, love, grace, and salvation. But the meaning behind those concepts will vary wildly depending on which church they're attending.

Take the word 'faith,' for example. The Bible talks about faith in terms of hope, trust, and dependence. It's believing and clinging to the promises of God, even when the circumstances of our lives make it difficult. Hebrews 11 reminds us that saints like Noah, Abraham, and Rahab trusted the Word of the Lord even when they couldn't see the final outcome of His promises. They believed that God would be true to His Word and keep His promises, and so they walked in obedience. A full *nineteen times* in Hebrews 11 alone, the author of Hebrews tells us that these men and women of God walked 'by faith.' As they did, they endured terrible suffering along the way.

In the Gospels, we see that faith is the posture of the heart that drives desperate people to Jesus. This is why Jesus so frequently told people that their *faith* had made them well (e.g., Mark 10:52, Luke 7:50). It wasn't that their faith possessed intrinsic power to heal them, if they only had the right amount. No, their faith healed them because it drove them to the One who could heal them. In conversations about the PG, it's *always* vital to remember that the intensity and integrity of a person's faith cannot save them; it's the object of faith that matters.

PG preachers talk about faith as a force with power outside of God Himself. Here's another Copeland quote: 'Faith was the raw material substance that the Spirit of God used to form the universe.'[5] Notice the assumption here. Faith is a *raw material*, which means it has a kind of creative power stored up in it. If that's true, then as believers exercise faith, they should also be able to shape reality and bring their desires to pass, just as the Lord did at creation. This is certainly not what the Bible teaches, and it leads to the creature/creator confusion we thought about earlier.

---

5 Jeff Klutz, *Apostasy! The Word-Faith Doctrinal Deception* (ReturningKing.com, 2012 [Kindle edition]), p. 60.

Such examples could be multiplied. According to Scripture, 'victory' isn't something that we accomplish, but something accomplished for us by the Lord Jesus (see 1 Cor. 15:55). But according to the PG, victory is something that we achieve as we conjure up enough faith and root out any lingering sin or doubt that may be hidden away in our hearts. When the PG preachers talk about the blessings God gives His people, they're almost always talking about physical and material ones—the health and the wealth. But the Bible points Christians to blessings that aren't primarily on this earth, but in the 'heavenly places' (Eph. 1:3). The Bible is far more interested in spiritual blessings than physical and material ones (e.g., Phil. 3:10, Col. 1:24).

While discussing the PG, definitions are always a problem. There are so many practitioners and varieties out there, and there's no accepted glossary of terms. It even goes by many names: the 'Word of Faith' movement, the 'health and wealth' gospel, the 'seed of faith.' Its advocates are the richest of the rich—and, sadly, the poorest of the poor. The famous and the unknown.

But wherever you see one or more of these found distinctives—God wants to bless you materially; God wants you to claim it; God wants you to be happy and never suffer; God wants you to prosper—you're probably dealing with the prosperity gospel. None of these are the real gospel.

And just so it's really clear to you, the real gospel you can summarize with the words *God, man, Christ,* and *response. God* is the good creator and ruler of all things. *Man* He created in His image to worship Him, but we rebelled and earned His just wrath. *Christ,* the Son of God, came to live the life we should have lived, died as a substitute to pay the penalty for sin, and rose from the grave defeating sin and death. Now, all who *respond* by repenting and following after Him in faith can be forgiven and given eternal life.

Friends, *that's* the gospel you, we, and all the world needs, not watered down imitations.

2. Excuse Me, But Your Bible is Upside Down

It's Sunday morning, and Joel Osteen is taking the stage at his Houston-based mega church. He's preparing to deliver a sermon to over ten million people, if you include online listeners and live attendees. Before the sermon begins, Osteen lifts his Bible high in the air and recites these now-iconic words:

This is my Bible.
I am what it says I am.
I can do what it says I can do.
Today, I will be taught the Word of God.
I boldly confess:
My mind is alert, my heart is receptive.
I will never be the same.
I am about to receive
The incorruptible, indestructible,
Ever-living seed of the Word of God.
I will never be the same.
Never, never, never.

I will never be the same.

In Jesus' name. Amen.[1]

There's nothing controversial or condemnable about this confession. In fact, on its face, it's quite commendable. We hope every genuine Christian would agree with every word of what we might call 'The Osteen Creed.' We are what the Bible says we are and we can *indeed* do what it says we can do. But this raises an important question: what does the Bible actually say about who we are and what we can do?

You can see why that's important, right?

We've already established that not everyone who quotes from the Bible is speaking God's truth. And that's why we need to talk about *hermeneutics*.

Don't let the big word scare you. Hermeneutics simply refers to how we read, interpret, and apply our Bibles. Your hermeneutic will help you determine whether Joel Osteen (or anyone else, for that matter) knows what he's talking about when he grabs a Bible and begins to tell you what to believe, think, and do.

Everyone who reads the Bible has a hermeneutic—a way of interpreting it. The question is whether their hermeneutic is good or bad, helpful or misleading. Here are six ways that PG teachers get the Bible wrong, whether intentionally or not. This may be the longest and densest chapter in the book, but it also may be the most important for equipping you to respond to the PG. So hang in there.

---

1   https://www.joelosteen.com/downloadables/Pages/Downloads/ThisIsMyBible_JOM.pdf Accessed October 12, 2019.

1. A Man-Centered Perspective

A few questions: Why does God do what He does? Why did He create the world with people in it? Why did He set His love on the people of Israel? Why does He forgive sin? What made Him love people enough to send Jesus to die on the cross and be raised from the dead for our salvation? Why does He bless His people and give them good gifts? Why does He intend to send Jesus back to judge the world and usher His people into a remade heaven and earth?

The Bible offers many answers to these questions. But one stands above all the rest: God does everything *for His own glory*. All of God's actions display His glorious character. When He blesses or judges or saves or delivers, He is showing the world who He is and what He is like. We could pile up hundreds of places in Scripture where we see this truth spelled out, but let's look at three for now:

In Isaiah 48, the Lord rebukes the people of Judah for their stubbornness and rebellion. But then He explains why He has chosen not to cut them off:

> For my name's sake I defer my anger;
>> for the sake of my praise I restrain it for you,
>> that I may not cut you off.
> Behold, I have refined you, but not as silver;
>> I have tried you in the furnace of affliction.
> For my own sake, for my own sake, I do it,
>> for how should my name be profaned?
>> My glory I will not give to another. (Isa. 48:9-11)

Centuries later, as Jesus approached the time of His crucifixion, He said:

Now is my soul troubled. And what shall I say? 'Father, save me from this hour'? But for this purpose I have come to this hour. Father, glorify your name. Then a voice came from heaven: 'I have glorified it, and I will glorify it again.' (John 12:27-28)

And a few decades after that, Paul reflected on the incredible blessings that all believers have in Christ:

Even as he chose us in him before the foundation of the world, that we should be holy and blameless before him. In love he predestined us for adoption to himself as sons through Jesus Christ, according to the purpose of his will, *to the praise of his glorious grace*, with which he has blessed us in the Beloved. (Eph. 1:4-6, emphasis added)

Why does God show mercy to sinful Judah? For the sake of His name and reputation. So that He might be known and loved and honored and praised for His incredible patience and kindness. Because He doesn't share His glory with anyone.

Why did Jesus willingly walk into the horror of the cross? Because He wanted to glorify His Father.

Why did He select us to be adopted into His family? So that His glorious grace might be praised.

Are you seeing the picture? God does what He does for His glory. Now, that might make God seem a bit vain and stuck-up. After all, we don't like people who make everything about themselves. That's because no mere human being is worthy of that kind of glory and praise. But God is not like man, and He actually deserves all glory and praise. He is wonderfully glorious, and so it's only right that He should want to display His glory. And it's only right that we should want to praise Him for doing so.

All this brings us to one of the major problems with the PG: by putting too much emphasis on God's gifts of health, success, and financial well-being, it places human beings at the center of the universe. But God won't share His glory with us, and His love and blessings are dispensed according to His own pleasure and for His own purposes—which, again, aren't focused on temporal pleasure.

2. Taking Verses Out of Context

Imagine for a moment that you have a co-worker who keeps one of those daily calendar devotionals on her desk. You know the kind I'm talking about, where every day you pull off a page and read the Scripture on the next page. Now imagine that one morning your co-worker pulls away a page to reveal a new Scripture. Today's Scripture is Matthew 4:9, which reads: 'All these things I will give you, if you will fall down and worship me.'

Your co-worker is encouraged by the verse. What a precious promise!

But you know your Bible a bit better than your co-worker. And so you know there's a problem with being encouraged by this verse. Why? Because Matthew 4:9 isn't a promise—nor is it an encouragement. It's actually a blasphemous temptation from Satan. So ... not exactly something that you would want to claim for yourself!

Here's the Golden Rule of reading and applying our Bibles correctly: always interpret a text in context. If your imaginary co-worker would have read Matthew 4:9 in its proper context, then she would have immediately realized that this verse isn't a sweet promise from God, but a lie from Satan.

Of course, it's not always this easy. PG preaching only makes sense if you continually take verses out of context. I (Sean) learned to read my Bible like this from my spiritual leaders. Every sermon I heard, every Bible study I attended, and every book I read reinforced this way of reading the Bible. My favorite out-of-context verse was Philippians 4:13. You probably know it, and it *is* a precious promise: 'I can do all things through him [Christ] who strengthens me.'

I quoted this verse hundreds of time. I read it in my Bible probably once or twice. And when I did, I never really paid much attention to the verses before or after Philippians 4:13.

If I would have taken the time to read the entire chapter, I would have seen that these verses are talking about Christ's ability to strengthen Paul for his ministry, which he needed precisely because Christ was allowing him to suffer greatly. The first clue to rightly interpreting verse 13 comes from the verse right before it. In verse 12, Paul writes about being 'brought low' and going hungry. Go back a little further, to chapter 3 verse 10, and you'll find him extolling the rich blessings of … *suffering*. Here's what he says:

> …that I may know him and the power of his resurrection, and may share his sufferings, becoming like him in his death.

Teachers of the prosperity gospel train their adherents to read verses out of context because actually reading Scripture in context reveals that blessings and brokenness usually go hand in hand. Here's another example:

> The Spirit himself bears witness with our spirit that we are children of God, and if children, then heirs—heirs of God and fellow heirs with Christ. (Rom. 8:16-17)

Wow.

Powerful.

Really strong stuff.

The PG told me this was a major 'go-to' verse when I needed to claim my blessings. 'I am a child of God,' I would say, 'and if I am a fellow heir with Christ, then all of the riches of Christ belong to me!' I said it because I believed it, and I believed it because I saw it in the Bible. And I 'saw it in the Bible' because so many preachers I heard would quote this verse as *proof* that God's Word promised me the fullness of material blessings.

Okay, but let's keep reading. Here's the rest of the verse, in context:

> The Spirit himself bears witness with our spirit that we are children of God, and if children, then heirs—heirs of God and fellow heirs with Christ, *provided we suffer with him* in order that we may also be glorified with him. (our emphasis)

Now that changes things.

First of all, a little context clearly reveals that the substance of our inheritance is our glorification in Christ. In other words, the promised blessing is spiritual, not material. Secondly, this sweet promise of glory is conditional. Here's what I mean: our glorification by Jesus comes after our suffering with Jesus. When I was steeped in the PG, I never even knew how that verse ended. Again, prosperity preachers know the only way they can use that verse for their aberrant theology is to rip it out of context, even its most immediate context.

3. Confusing the Covenants

The Bible is divided up into two parts, the Old Testament and the New Testament. The Old Testament records events from the creation of the world up until roughly 400 years before the birth of Christ. It tells us how God called the nation of Israel to be His people, and how Israel repeatedly broke the covenant (agreement) that God made with them. The New Testament begins right before the birth of Jesus and tells us about His life, death, resurrection, and ascension; it then narrates the events that led to the establishment of the Christian Church.

As we think about interpreting the Bible, we need to realize the important differences between the people of God in the Old Covenant and the people of God in the New Covenant. For example, under the Old Covenant, inclusion in God's people meant you were born into a particular nation (Israel) and a particular family (the descendants of Abraham). In other words, you were born into God's family. But in the New Covenant, God's people is no longer Israel, but the Church. This difference is crucial. The people of God are those who have repented of their sins and trusted in God's Son Jesus for salvation (Jer. 31:31-34, Heb. 10:16-17). In short, the New Covenant Church isn't a particular nation or ethnic group or family. It's a spiritual family, comprised of people from every tribe, tongue, people, and nation—those who were once strangers are now siblings through their mutual faith in the Lord Jesus. The Old Covenant always anticipated this transition, and it came to fruition through Jesus Christ.

This might sound irrelevant and overly technical. But it's important because the Old Testament is full of God's specific promises to the nation of Israel. Many of these promises relate to physical and material blessings that would come to them as they were faithful to the specific terms of the specific covenant that God had made with them.

For example, look at Deuteronomy 28:

> And if you faithfully obey the voice of the LORD your God, being careful to do all his commandments that I command you today, the LORD your God will set you high above all the nations of the earth…. And the LORD will make you abound in prosperity, in the fruit of your womb and in the fruit of your livestock and in the fruit of your ground, within the land that the LORD swore to your fathers to give you. The LORD will open to you his good treasury, the heavens, to give the rain to your land in its season and to bless all the work of your hands. And you shall lend to many nations, but you shall not borrow. (Deut. 28:1, 11-12)

God's promised blessings to His Old Covenant people were conditional ('if you faithfully obey'), material, and immediate. If you obey Him, He will bless you materially—now. In the New Testament, however, the emphasis shifts as does the timeline of fulfillment. There are material promises.

For instance, Paul looks forward to the day when the curse is removed from creation and from our bodies (see Rom. 8:19-23). But the fulfillment of those material promises is pushed back in the timeline of history—to Jesus' return. Meanwhile, the New Testament wants to shift our attention from *that* stuff to what folk might call the spiritual stuff (e.g., Acts 14:22, Rom. 8:17, Jude 20-23).

Why is that? Well, it goes back to what's 'new' about the New Covenant. At different points, the people of God under the Old Testament had all the material blessings anyone could ask for. Think of Israel at the time of Solomon, say in 1 Kings chapter 10 when royalty from around the world come to admire Solomon and the kingdom's splendor. Talk about the golden days. Chapter 10 was it! Yet was that splendor enough to save Israel and keep them faithful? If you're determined to think so, you had better not read chapter 11 and following.

The lesson of the whole Old Testament and all those conditional promises, in other words, is to teach us that our problems are not fundamentally material or physical. Our problem is fundamentally spiritual. We have rejected God, His provision, and His rule over our lives. We don't want to overstate the case: God certainly does bless His New Covenant people materially in some ways. But the heart of His concerns and promises—at this moment of history—are spiritual (Ephesians 1:3ff), not material.

The PG tends to ignore the difference between the Old Covenant and the New. Many of its teachers point to the material promises made to the Old Covenant people of God *as if they were promises for New Covenant believers.* But they're not. These preachers will say things like, 'God's promises cannot be broken!' That's true. God's promises can't be broken, but they can be fulfilled. And in Christ, all of the promises of the Old Testament find their fulfillment (Matt. 5:17, 2 Cor. 1:20). We simply can't take a promise made to an Israelite under the Old Covenant about their healthy livestock, and apply it directly to our twenty-first-century bank accounts.

4. Mixing Up the Timeline

This error is related to the last. Some promises in Scripture will never be fulfilled in this life; Christians must wait until they arrive on the other side of eternity. For example, consider the promise of perfect health. We can be sure that there *will be a day* when God will make a new heaven and new earth—and as a result, all pain, tears, and sadness will be eradicated (Rev. 21:1-4). But nowhere does God promise that we'll enjoy perfect health in this life.

Now, if you've been around the PG for a while, you might be wondering: what about Isaiah 53:5? Aren't we told 'with his wounds we are healed'? Yes, we are. Matthew's Gospel even applies it to physical healing (Matt. 8:17). But both Isaiah's prophesy and the miraculous healings of Jesus' ministry pointed to the spiritual healing we all need. Peter draws out this lesson for churches: 'He himself bore our sins in his body on the tree, so that we might die to sin and live to righteousness. By his wounds you have been healed' (1 Pet. 2:24).

Jesus died to cure the sin-sickness of our souls. The healing He purchased for us has to do with sin and righteousness, not cancer or the common cold. (By the way, this illustrates an important principle for biblical interpretation: when possible, we want to let the Bible tell us what the Bible means.)

In fact, the only place in Scripture where believers are promised perfect physical health is found in 1 Corinthians 15:42-53. You can read the entire section on your own, but here's a little snapshot: '[The body] is sown in dishonor; it is raised in glory. It is sown in weakness; it is raised in power. It is sown a natural body; it is raised a spiritual body' (1 Cor. 15:43-44). Our escape from the 'weakness' of our bodies (i.e. sickness, injuries, the ravages of old age, etc.) will only happen when it is finally 'sown,' that is, when we die and God 'raises' us in power with a new, spiritual body.

Our perishable bodies will pass away, and when they do we'll put on imperishable bodies that we've all longed for. It will happen in 'the twinkling of an eye' (1 Cor. 15:52), when the trumpet sounds. But until that day, we continue to inhabit these mortal bodies, ravaged by the effects of the Fall.

It's true that I am what the Bible says I am, but the Bible says I'm made of dust. And it's true that I can do what the Bible says I can do, but the Bible doesn't tell me I can undo the effects of the Fall here and now. Instead it tells me that I must wait patiently, trusting the Lord will keep me until the day when He makes all things new.

5. Reading Proverbs as Promises

Every Christian parent tries to lead and love their children in the discipline and instruction of the Lord (Eph. 6:4). So when we read a verse like Proverbs 22:6, we want to claim it as a promise in the most literal sense: 'Train up a child in the way he should go; even when he is old he will not depart from it' (Prov. 22:6).

It might seem like this proverb means that if we do our part as a parent, God will do His part and save our kids. But it's important to remember that proverbs aren't absolute promises. They are more like maxims; they communicate general truths in memorable ways.

So Proverbs 22:6 isn't a promise that God will bless all good parenting by saving all good parents' children. It's a general truth that good parents who faithfully show their children what it looks like to follow Jesus will see their children follow in their footsteps. But, of course, in a fallen world, that's not always the case. Sometimes, children are trained well by their parents and they still go 'off the rails.'

PG preachers love to proclaim proverbs about prosperity and health as if they were absolute promises. Generally speaking, it's true that if we work hard, exercise self-control, and practice good stewardship, we will prosper financially. But sometimes in this life, lazy people get all the breaks and hard-working people struggle to make ends meet. See Ecclesiastes 8:14 or Psalm 73 for a mediation on just how unfair life can seem sometimes. We can't read proverbial wisdom as if it offers an unbreakable promise.

6. Misunderstanding the Reciprocity Principle

The 'reciprocity principle' goes something like this: if I do good, then God will bless me. If I do bad, then God will curse me. This is the way Job's friends saw the world.

When they saw their friend suffering, they wrongly assumed he must have offended the Lord (see Job 4:7-9 for one example). But the Bible is full of righteous people who suffer—like Jeremiah, Paul, and Jesus—and wicked people who prosper—like Jeroboam, the wicked king used by the Lord to restore the borders of Israel in 2 Kings 14:23-27.

In the New Testament, Jesus' disciples make the same mistake as Job's friends. They see a man who was born blind, so they asked Jesus whether the blind man's sin or his parents' sin caused his condition (John 9:1-2). They had a simplistic 'on/off' hermeneutic: bad behavior brings curses and good behavior brings blessings. So, obviously, anyone born blind must have done something to deserve it.

Thankfully, Jesus corrects His disciples' error: 'It was not that this man sinned, or his parents, but that the works of God might be displayed in him' (John 9:3). Turns out, this man's condition had nothing to do with any specific sin or pattern of sin. God made this man blind so that Jesus might heal him and, by healing him, display the works of God.

In this chapter, we've looked at some common missteps PG teachers make as they misinterpret and misapply the Bible. Perhaps it seems like we're nit-picking, but these errors aren't small. As Christians, we should be committed to believing that we are what the Bible says we are and we can do what the Bible says we can do. That's precisely why we must understand what God really says in His Word.

3. Yeah, But What About the Promises of Health and Happiness?

Have you ever felt the floor fall out from underneath you? Perhaps in the middle of a debate or an argument?

I (Sean) have, and it's unpleasant.

Moments like these are rarely the result of some cataclysmic event. They rarely happen after finishing a powerful book or listening through an extraordinary sermon series. Rather, they tend to happen after a single sentence or turn of a phrase. Someone says *just* the right thing in *just* the right way at *just* the right time and, in a moment, the penny drops, the lights go on, and your whole way of thinking goes up in smoke.

A moment like this led me to abandon the PG. Here's how it happened: I was having a conversation with a fellow believer, and I was arguing that Jesus' death purchased complete physical healing—without exception—for all believers. We only needed the faith to believe it.

I won't recount the entire debate, but you should know I really threw the kitchen sink at this guy. I gave him the best of my bad metaphors, silly syllogisms, and illogical illustrations. I was quoting Scripture and taking verses out of context like Steven Seagal taking out bad guys. As the argument came to a close, no one had changed their mind, but I went to bed that night confident I had won the battle. Little did I know, the war had only just begun.

The next morning, I spent my devotional time studying healing (of course!). And then it happened: the floor fell out from underneath me. I was reading 1 Corinthians 12, and I came across these words:

> And God has appointed in the church first apostles, second prophets, third teachers, then miracles, then gifts of healing, helping, administrating, and various kinds of tongues. Are all apostles? Are all prophets? Are all teachers? Do all work miracles? Do all possess gifts of healing? (1 Cor. 12:28-30)

Paul's rhetorical question clearly indicated that not everyone has the ability to heal. So, if access to healing is available to all believers, then why would the gift of healing be limited to a certain group?

A bomb had just fallen on my theological playground. The clarity of God's Word cut through the fog and brought me to the truth.

In the next two chapters, we want to point out some places in Scripture that stand directly against the claims of the PG. They will be helpful for anyone thinking through the PG's claims. We're convinced that Scripture is clear, and so it's fairly simple to show that the PG is unbiblical. We'll consider three of its core beliefs:

1. Christ's work gives all believers access through faith to physical healing.
2. Suffering is not meant to be a part of the Christian life.
3. God wills for His people to be materially prosperous.

We'll tackle the first two in this chapter, and the third in the next.

Before we get into the Bible, we should remind you to take note of the posture of your heart. Pride, fear, and stubbornness are powerful emotions. They make it difficult to admit we might have been wrong. So we urge you to pray as you read these passages, asking the Holy Spirit to open eyes, soften hearts, and reveal the truth.

Should Christians Expect Physical Healing?

We talked about Isaiah 53:5 a little bit in the previous chapter, but it's worth looking at more in depth here. It is probably safe to say that if you were to walk into any PG church on any given Sunday, you will hear, 'But he was pierced for our transgressions, he was crushed for our iniquities; the punishment that brought us peace was on him, and by his wounds we are healed' (Isa. 53:5, NIV).

When I (Sean) was in the military, we used to talk about taking out bad guys with precision: one shot, one kill. That's kind of how Isaiah 53:5 works in the minds of PG proponents. Just read the text; it's right there. It's not complicated: by His wounds, we are healed. Don't overthink it.

Perhaps you've had this verse quoted to you while you were wrestling with a cold. Maybe you've even quoted this verse yourself when praying for someone to be healed of cancer. Or maybe you've found yourself in a debate with someone subsumed by the PG and no matter how you try and redirect the conversation, it always seems to come back to this idea. It's hard to overstate the way in which Isaiah 53:5 serves as a lynchpin verse for the PG. So it's really important to understand what God is saying there.

We could say a lot about Isaiah 53:5 and its context. The 'suffering servant' song of Isaiah 52:13–53:12 is among Scripture's most moving and powerful passages. But in order to help future conversations not get too bogged down in the details, let's turn again to the New Testament.

In the last chapter, we said it's always best to let the Bible interpret itself. Thankfully, we don't have to guess or argue about what Isaiah 53:5 means. Why? Because the same Holy Spirit who inspired Isaiah to write it also inspired the apostle Peter to tell us what it means. Look for yourself: 'He himself bore our sins in his body on the tree, that we might die to sin and live to righteousness. By his wounds you have been healed' (1 Pet. 2:24).

In context, Peter is teaching his readers about the significance of Jesus' death. On the cross—or 'the tree,' to use Peter's words—Jesus 'bore our sins.' In other words, He stood in our place as our substitute, taking on Himself the sin and guilt of His people. Peter was a Jewish man who would have known his Old Testament well, and so it comes as no surprise that contemplating Jesus' suffering on the cross reminded him of Isaiah 53. And so he summarizes the point of Jesus' death by quoting Isaiah's song. Jesus endured all of that suffering, Peter tells us, so that we might be healed by His wounds.

None of this is controversial. PG's practitioners and critics would agree. But the disagreement arises over the nature of the healing that comes to us through His wounds. Is it spiritual healing or physical healing?

This is a great question. But rather than argue about it, let's just let Peter tell us. He says Jesus bore our sins 'that we might die to sin and live to righteousness.' Scripture's clarity is helpful here: Jesus died so that sin might be killed in us, and righteousness might live in us. Does that sound like physical or spiritual healing to you? Peter understands Jesus' death on the cross as a matter of sin and righteousness, not chest colds and cancer.

This alone deals a serious blow to one of the most commonly used PG pretexts. But there are other really good reasons to reject the notion that Christ's work on the cross somehow secures physical healing for all believers. Consider:

- There has been a 100 per cent mortality rate for Christians over the past 2,000 years. This happens to be exactly the same mortality of unbelievers. The death of Christ seems to have had exactly no impact on the final physical health of His followers. If Jesus' wounds purchased our healing, then He's at best a short-term Savior whose deliverance expires when we need it most.

- James tells sick Christians to go to the elders for prayer (James 5:15). Why would he do that if healing were the right of every blood-bought believer?

- Paul tells Timothy to 'use a little wine for the sake of (his) stomach and your frequent ailments' (1 Tim. 5:23). Why would he do that if Timothy just needed more faith? If Paul was ever going to tell someone to claim healing for themselves, then surely it would have been his 'beloved son' Timothy (2 Tim. 1:2). But Paul doesn't seem to believe that Timothy's lack of faith is blocking his healing pipeline. Instead, he seems to believe Timothy just needs some medicine (see also 2 Tim. 4:20).

Hopefully you get the point. Did Jesus' death purchase our physical healing? In one sense, sure. Jesus died to secure our salvation, which includes the final resurrection and glorification of our bodies in eternity (1 Cor. 15:50-53). But that only happens after we die, and we usually die because we get sick—whether we're twenty, fifty, or one hundred years old. God may graciously choose to heal our infirmities until then, and we ought to pray for those who are suffering physically. But we cannot expect that we will always receive healing in this life.

Is Suffering Incompatible With a Faithful Life?

I (Sean) once heard a pastor say that it's up to us how long we remain in suffering. The choice is ours: trial or triumph. We can choose to remain in a state of suffering, or at any moment we can exercise our faith and claim victory over our circumstances and rise up victorious like Jesus in the resurrection.

It's true that Jesus had that kind of power and authority (e.g., Matt. 26:53 and Matt. 28:18). But should we expect that same kind of control?

Can we disentangle ourselves from the suffering that ensnares us at any given moment? Let's look at the lives of three people in the Bible and try to answer those questions.

Paul – Suffering for the Glory of Christ
The apostle Paul didn't believe his faith made him immune to suffering. In fact, when some of his opponents demanded that he defend his credentials as a leader, he didn't hold up his victorious life of abundance and his ability to conquer challenges. Instead, he did the opposite. Look at what he wrote to the church at Corinth:

> Are they servants of Christ? I am a better one ... with far greater labors, far more imprisonments, with countless beatings, and often near death. Five times I received at the hands of the Jews the forty lashes less one. Three times I was beaten with rods. Once I was stoned. Three times I was shipwrecked; a night and a day I was adrift at sea; on frequent journeys, in danger from rivers, danger from robbers, danger from my own people, danger from Gentiles, danger in the city, danger in the wilderness, danger at sea, danger from false brothers; in toil and hardship, through many a sleepless night, in hunger and thirst, often without food, in cold and exposure. And, apart from other things, there is the daily pressure on me of my anxiety for all the churches. Who is weak, and I am not weak? Who is made to

fall, and I am not indignant? If I must boast, I will boast of the things that show my weakness. (2 Cor. 11:23-30)

Paul believed that his suffering *actually qualified him as a servant of Christ*. When Jesus called Paul into His service (Acts 9:1-16), He called him to suffer. Paul's conversion didn't miraculously give him the power to rebuke his troubles and speak blessing into existence. He couldn't pass from tragedy to triumph by sheer force of will. What's more, Jesus wasn't ambiguous about this. When Jesus sent a man named Ananias to go and get Paul, here's what He said, 'For I will show him how much he must suffer for the sake of my name' (Acts 9:16).

Rather than trying to remove himself from his suffering, Paul embraced it. We're not saying Paul *enjoyed* his troubles, but he understood them as part and parcel of following Jesus. Moreover, Paul could rejoice in his suffering. (2 Cor. 12:10) Remember the context of everyone's favorite verse? 'Not that I am speaking of being in need, for I have learned in whatever situation I am to be content. I know how to be brought low, and I know how to abound. In any and every circumstance, I have learned the secret of facing plenty and hunger, abundance and need. I can do all things through him who strengthens me' (Phil. 4:11-13). For Paul, Christian triumph wasn't a matter of escaping trials, but learning how to glorify God as he endured them.

It wasn't just Paul who shared this vision of the Christian life. When the apostles were arrested and beaten by the religious authorities, we read: 'Then they left the presence of the council, rejoicing that they were counted worthy to suffer dishonor for the name' (Acts 5:41).

Don't believe the lie that this call to suffer is only for apostles or otherwise 'Super Christians.' Ordinary Christians like you and me ought to expect the same:

> For it has been granted to you that for the sake of Christ you should not only believe in him but also suffer for his sake, engaged in the same conflict that you saw I had and now hear that I still have. (Phil. 1:29-30)

> In this you rejoice, though now for a little while, if necessary, you have been grieved by various trials. (1 Pet. 1:6)

> But recall the former days when, after you were enlightened, you endured a hard struggle with sufferings, sometimes being publicly exposed to reproach and affliction, and sometimes being partners with those so treated. (Heb. 10:32-33)

> But even if you should suffer for righteousness' sake, you will be blessed. Have no fear of them, nor be troubled. (1 Pet. 3:14)

> The Spirit himself bears witness with our spirit that we are children of God, and if children, then heirs—heirs of God and fellow heirs with Christ, provided we suffer with him in order that we may also be glorified with him. (Rom. 8:16-17)

> Do not fear what you are about to suffer. Behold, the devil is about to throw some of you into prison, that you may be tested, and for ten days you will have tribulation. Be faithful unto death, and I will give you the crown of life. (Rev. 2:10)

If anyone would come after me, let him deny himself and take up his cross and follow me. (Mark 8:34)

When you read through that list, do you come away with the impression that God's will is for His children to be spared trouble and hardship in this life? Do these passages teach us to expect that faithfulness will always bring about financial prosperity, physical health, and relational ease? The Bible teaches us that suffering is a tool that God uses to grow, teach, and shape us (cf., 2 Cor. 12:7, Rom. 5:3-5).

Job – the Righteous Sufferer

Perhaps the biggest chink in the armor of the PG is the Old Testament book of Job. It's a long book, but you should read it—all forty-two chapters' worth! For our purposes, however, you don't need to have read the whole book. We just want to highlight three things.

1. Job was righteous.

In saying this, we don't mean that Job was sinless. We simply mean that he was an upright man. While still a sinner, he had oriented his life toward the worship and obedience of God, and love for those around him. We see this clear as day in the first verse: 'There was a man in the land of Uz whose name was Job, and that man was blameless and upright, one who feared God and turned away from evil' (Job 1:1).

2. It was the will of the Lord for Job to suffer.

If you don't know the story, mark your page in this book and go read the first two chapters of Job. This upright man lost his home, his livestock, his health, and his children. And after all that, his wife scorned him. While it's certainly true that Satan was responsible for this suffering, it's equally true that God stood sovereignly over the mayhem (Job 1:12). Like the blind man in John 9, these things didn't happen to Job because he was wicked or because he didn't have enough faith. They happened because God's will for his life involved great trials.

3. Job glorified God in the midst of his suffering.

It's difficult to think clearly when we're in the midst of great pain. But Job seemed to have clarity all along. He knew his suffering was a part of God's good plan for his life. Rather than cursing God for his pain (Job 2:9) or trying to understand the silver lining in the dark clouds, Job endured this great trial, even if imperfectly, and glorified God in the process. At one point, he declared, 'Though he slay me, I will hope in him' (Job 13:15).

PG preachers say that those with a sufficiently robust faith will earn freedom from suffering. But that wasn't true for Job. Because he found his greatest hope *not* in the absence of any suffering, but in the presence of his God. His faith didn't answer every question, but it did address the most important ones. Even when suffering came, Job understood that it came from the hand of God, and through the deepest possible pain, he found hope in the God who 'slayed' him.

But Job is not the only righteous man in the Bible to be slayed by God.

Jesus – the Suffering Servant.

If you are a Christian, then you surely believe Jesus never sinned. The New Testament is clear: He 'knew no sin'

(2 Cor. 5:21), He 'committed no sin' (1 Pet. 2:22), and He was 'without sin' (Heb. 4:15).

And yet, Jesus suffered terribly. He was born in poverty, betrayed by a friend, condemned by His countrymen, beaten by religious leaders, mocked by soldiers, abandoned by His closest confidants, and ultimately murdered by the most powerful empire on earth. As He hung on the cross in shame and agony, He endured the justice of God that we deserve for our sin (1 John 2:2).

None of this happened by chance. The Bible plainly tells us that it was the will of the Father for the Son:

> Yet it was the will of the LORD to crush him; he has put him to grief. (Isa. 53:10a)

> From that time Jesus began to show his disciples *that he must go to Jerusalem and suffer many things* from the elders and chief priests and scribes, and be killed, and on the third day be raised. (Matt. 16:21, our emphasis)

> This Jesus, *delivered up according to the definite plan and foreknowledge of God,* you crucified and killed by the hands of lawless men. (Acts 2:23, our emphasis)

> For truly in this city there were gathered together against your holy servant Jesus, whom you anointed, both Herod and Pontius Pilate, along with the Gentiles and the peoples of Israel, *to do whatever your hand and your plan had predestined to take place.* (Acts 4:27-28, our emphasis)

It's fairly simple. If even the perfectly faithful Son of God suffered, then faithful people will suffer. Now, maybe you reply, 'Well, that's Jesus. He was *supposed* to suffer. That was His role—He suffered so I don't have to.' In one sense, that's true. Jesus suffered the penalty for our sins so that we *not* suffer that penalty. He swallowed God's wrath so that we might receive God's righteousness (2 Cor. 5:21). But when we're talking about physical and earthly suffering, nowhere does God tell us that Jesus took that from us. In fact, the New Testament tells us to *expect* that kind of suffering.

> For what credit is it if, when you sin and are beaten for it, you endure? But if when you do good and suffer for it you endure, this is a gracious thing in the sight of God. For to this you have been called, because Christ also suffered for you, *leaving you an example*, so that you might follow in his steps. (1 Pet. 2:20-21)

You can't follow Jesus without walking in His steps. Suffering in our life isn't a sign that something has gone wrong; it's more likely a sign that we're walking the same road Jesus walked.

4. Yeah, But What About the Promises of Wealth?

We've already seen that Jesus' death doesn't secure physical healing in this life for believers; we've also seen that God sometimes wills for His people to suffer. Now onto our third question:

Does God Will for His People to be Materially Prosperous?

We all like money. If you found a $100 bill stuck into the next page of this book, you certainly wouldn't turn it down! And so it's tempting to see the PG preachers on TV, with their fancy suits and private jets, and think, 'Man, they must be doing something right!' When we hear them say that God wants us to be rich just like they are, well, we figure we must be doing something wrong, since we're still flying Economy.

Our God is a good and gracious Father, and He is happy to provide for our physical needs (see Matt. 6:25-34). It's also true that following biblical principles regarding work, thrift, and money will generally lead to financial well-being.

But it simply isn't true that God means for His people to be rich. It's not true that God will reward our generosity through our bank balance. It's not true that faithful followers of Jesus cannot experience poverty. Many PG preachers say otherwise by twisting a few verses out of context. But we'd like to go straight to the source.

Here are three clear biblical principles that lead us to reject the PG.

1. Money can be dangerous.

Could you imagine someone pleading with the Lord not to give him too much money? That might sound crazy, but that's exactly what Agur son of Jakeh does in the book of Proverbs. Here's what he says to the Lord:

> Two things I ask of you; deny them not to me before I die: Remove far from me falsehood and lying; give me neither poverty nor riches; feed me with the food that is needful for me, lest I be full and deny you and say, 'Who is the LORD?' or lest I be poor and steal and profane the name of my God. (Prov. 30:7-9)

Let's unpack that. Agur desperately wants two things from God. First, he wants the Lord to keep him from falsehood and lying. So far, so good. We expect the Bible to say stuff like that. Then Agur asks the Lord not to give him poverty. That also makes sense. But then he keeps going. And what he says next is shocking. He asks the Lord to keep him from … riches.

If you've bought into the PG, this request makes no sense at all. If we measure God's blessings in terms of bank balances and luxury vehicles, then why would we ever ask for *less*? Thankfully, Agur explains his thinking in verse 9: he's afraid that if he becomes rich, he might be tempted to be self-reliant and forget the Lord.

This is a very important piece of the Bible's teaching about money. And frankly, it's one the PG preachers ignore because they cannot explain it away. To be sure, material wealth is a blessing in many ways, but it's also very dangerous. This is the ruin of the rich man in Jesus' parable—he's content to be rich in crops and barns, but not toward God (Luke 12:21).

Money can also distract people from their walk with the Lord to their ultimate spiritual destruction. Jesus refers to this in His parable of the sower and the seeds. Some of the plants sprung up only for a moment. Why? Because they get choked out by the 'deceitfulness of riches' (Matt. 13:22). As Paul writes to Timothy:

> But those who desire to be rich fall into temptation, into a snare, into many senseless and harmful desires that plunge people into ruin and destruction. For the love of money is a root of all kinds of evils. It is through this craving that some have wandered away from the faith and pierced themselves with many pangs. (1 Tim. 6:9-10)

This is one of the reasons the PG leads people into great spiritual danger. By encouraging people to long for riches, it places a snare in their path. The Bible says it's not worth it. It's far better to be poor and aware of your dependence on the Lord than to be rich and deceived into thinking you don't need Him.

2. We See Examples of Faithful Poor People in the Bible.

If the PG is correct, then you should be able to measure your faithfulness based on how much the Lord has chosen to bless you materially. But if faithful prayers are answered with financial blessings, then how do we explain the poor people in the Bible who are praised for their faithfulness? Just look at a few examples:

Ruth. When we first meet Ruth, she's a young widow about to move to a foreign country. Once she arrives in Bethlehem, she's so destitute that she picks up scraps in the fields in order to have enough to eat. According to the PG, those who are 'in good' with God should never experience these kinds of harrowing difficulties. But it's clear that Ruth is being held up as a model of faithfulness (e.g., Ruth 2:11).

The poor widow. Luke's Gospel records Jesus as He observed people giving money in the temple:

> Jesus looked up and saw the rich putting their gifts into the offering box, and he saw a poor widow put in two small copper coins. And he said, 'Truly, I tell you, this poor widow has put in more than all of them. For they all contributed out of their abundance, but she out of her poverty put in all she had to live on.' (Luke 21:1-4)

According to the logic of the PG, we would expect Jesus to call out the wealthy for their faithfulness. They obviously knew about the law of sowing and reaping because they were sowing their financial seeds and reaping the rewards in their bank balances! But surprisingly, Jesus points to the poor woman as a model of faith. He commends her complete love for and trust in the Lord, for she was willing to part with all of her meager resources.

The Macedonian church. In 2 Corinthians, Paul urged the church to give generously for the relief of the famine-stricken church in Jerusalem. In doing so, he held out the churches in Macedonia as an example of generosity:

> We want you to know, brothers, about the grace of God that has been given among the churches of Macedonia, or in a severe test of affliction, their abundance of joy and their extreme poverty have overflowed in a wealth of generosity on their part. For they gave according to their means, as I can testify, and beyond their means, of their own accord, begging us earnestly for the favor of taking part in the relief of the saints— and this, not as we expected, but they gave themselves first to the Lord and then by the will of God to us.' (2 Cor. 8:1-5)

According to the principles of the PG, we would expect that they had experienced great financial increase as a result of their great love for the Lord. But in fact, Paul highlights their abundance of joy and *their extreme poverty*. The idea of 'joyful poverty' makes no sense to PG preachers. But that's only because they don't know what the Macedonians knew—that it is better to have the Lord than great riches!

It's important to notice that the faithfulness of these poor people doesn't seem to be rooted in a desire to be rich. They didn't love the Lord in the hopes that He would make them rich. They loved the Lord in their great poverty because He was their great treasure. It's clear that the Bible severs the PG's connection between faith and wealth.

3. The Bible Says the Poor are Particularly the Objects of God's Love.

Throughout the Old Testament, God instructs the people of Israel to care for the poor (e.g., Lev. 19:19-20, Deut. 15:7-8). These commands are rooted in God's own character, for He is personally interested in the plight of the needy (e.g., Ps. 140:12, Prov. 14:31). Despite those facts, however, in Jesus' day it was commonly thought that being rich was a sign that God favored you (sound familiar?).

But Jesus repeatedly blew that idea up because He understood that the arrival of God's salvation was particularly good news for the poor (Luke 4:18). We've already seen how Jesus valued the smaller gift of the poor widow. But that's not the only time Jesus upends conventional wisdom. Here are a few examples:

> And he lifted up his eyes on his disciples, and said: Blessed are you who are poor, for yours is the kingdom of God.... But woe to you who are rich, for you have received your consolation. (Luke 6:20 and 6:24)

> And Jesus said to his disciples, 'Truly, I say to you, only with difficulty will a rich person enter the kingdom of heaven. Again I tell you, it is easier for a camel to go through the eye of a needle than for a rich person to enter the kingdom of God.' (Matt. 19:23-24)

If you examine Jesus' parables, you'll see that rich people were often used as negative examples. It's as if Jesus is warning His hearers *not* to be like them. Think of the unnamed wealthy man in the Parable of Lazarus and the Rich Man (Luke

16:19-31) or the unwise landowner in the Parable of the Rich Fool (Luke 12:16-21). Both show us how wealth can lead someone to live with presumption and pride.

The book of Revelation also offers an interesting contrast along these lines. In Revelation 2–3, we read seven letters written by Jesus to ancient churches. For our purposes, let's look at the church at Laodicea. It seems they were financially well off. But look at how Jesus addresses them:

> For you say, I am rich, I have prospered, and I need nothing, not realizing that you are wretched, pitiable, poor, blind, and naked. I counsel you to buy from me gold refined by fire, so that you may be rich, and white garments so that you may clothe yourself and the shame of your nakedness may not be seen, and salve to anoint your eyes, so that you may see. Those whom I love, I reprove and discipline, so be zealous and repent.' (Rev. 3:17-19)

Laodicea's wealth had blinded them to their spiritual state. They'd grown lukewarm in their faith (Rev. 3:15-16), but thought they needed nothing. But spiritually speaking, they were pitiable and poor. They needed to change immediately, and so Jesus urged them to turn and 'buy' what they needed from Him.

Contrast His words to the church in Laodicea to His words to the church in Smyrna. Here's what Jesus says to the Symrnans:

> I know your tribulation and your poverty (but you are rich) and the slander of those who say that they are Jews and are not, but are a synagogue of Satan. Do not fear what you are about to suffer. Behold, the devil is about to throw some of

you into prison, that you may be tested, and for ten days you will have tribulation. Be faithful unto death, and I will give you the crown of life.' (Rev. 2:9-10)

Smyrna found itself in the opposite situation as Laodicea. They were in poverty and facing persecution. But Jesus saw them differently as well. To Him, though they were materially poor, they were *rich* because they remained faithful despite their suffering. He knew their life was difficult, but He promised them it would be worth it in the end. Imagine how the 'name it and claim it' crowd would instruct this kind of church! Instead of praising them and telling them to endure their suffering, they'd probably curse them for not believing God's Word. After all, they *should be* experiencing their best life now!

Responding properly to the gospel requires humility. No person can come to Jesus in faith unless they realize they're not OK on their own. But wealth may obscure this. It makes it easier to fool ourselves into thinking we don't need any help. When we have a lot of money, it's a lot harder to 'leave it all' and follow Jesus. People mired in poverty don't have those same disadvantages. The call to leave everything now for a future reward may not seem quite as scary for them, for they have 'less' to lose.

This is why the book of James says such radically different things about the poor and the rich:

Listen, my beloved brothers, has not God chosen those who are poor in the world to be rich in faith and heirs of the kingdom, which he has promised to those who love him? (James 2:5)

Come now, you rich, weep and howl for the miseries that are coming upon you. Your riches have rotted and your garments are moth-eaten. Your gold and silver have corroded, and their corrosion will be evidence against you and will eat your flesh like fire. You have laid up treasure in the last days. (James 5:1-3)

Don't misunderstand. James is *not* saying that being poor automatically gets you closer to heaven. Poverty isn't noble in and of itself. There are plenty of wicked poor people, and plenty of godly people with money. But being rich in this life is merely a temporary blessing, and it's one that makes it less likely you will come to Jesus and be 'rich in faith.' It is insane to store up material wealth as if the day of judgment will never come. After all, on that day God will give the kingdom to those who love Him—not those who have hoarded riches for themselves.

We hope that this overview has convinced you that the PG can't account for the Bible's teaching. You simply can't square the idea that God wants you to be wealthy with the fact that the Bible says so many positive things about the poor and gives so many warnings to the rich. Money is dangerous. The faithful are sometimes (often?) poor. God loves the humble and lowly, so the poor have the inside track.

The PG comes to us with a twisted message that might initially seem like good news: God wants to make you rich and successful! But it's a message that doesn't deliver, and you probably know that deep down inside. Most people who send money to PG ministries will never get rich, and even if they did that doesn't mean that they will be happy. One hundred per cent of them will get sick and die eventually. And then what will all of the naming and claiming get them?

But the gospel of Jesus, the one that the Bible teaches, is really and truly good news. There is treasure, but it's not the kind that moths and rust can destroy; it's not the kind of treasure that you leave behind when you die. Jesus wants to make us rich towards God and load our arms with an inheritance that will never perish.

5. Do TBN Viewers Go to Heaven?

The man who discipled me (Sean) in the PG was like a father to me. He loved me when not many people did. He opened up his home to me when I had no home to call my own. He helped me financially when I struggled to make ends meet. So when I came to understand that the prosperity gospel was so far from the message that Jesus and the apostles proclaimed, I wondered what that meant for this man who had loved me so well when I so desperately needed it.

Could it be that he wasn't really a Christian?

Perhaps you've wrestled with a similar question. You're thinking about a pastor you know, or a relative. You're trying to figure out an answer. If everything we're saying is true, then that means the PG is a false gospel. So what does that mean for your dad who's all-in on Creflo Dollar, or your wife who loves reading Joel Osteen, or your friend who listens to Paula White and Joyce Meyer?

In other words, 'Do people who watch TBN go to heaven?' If you don't know TBN, it's the Trinity Broadcast

Network, an American cable channel known for featuring prosperity preachers. Of course, watching a TV channel isn't the issue. Here's a more straightforward and better way to ask the question: Do people who *embrace the message of the prosperity gospel* go to heaven?

This is a difficult, yet important question. We must look to the Bible for help. In the end, it only matters what God says on any given subject, so we must commit ourselves to listening to His Word rather than our feelings or preferences.

Let's begin by asking a fundamental question: what is a Christian?

What is a Christian?

First things first: not everyone who *says* they're a follower of Jesus really *is* a follower of Jesus. Consider these passages:

> Not everyone who says to me, 'Lord, Lord,' will enter the kingdom of heaven, but the one who does the will of my Father who is in heaven. (Matt. 7:21)

> What good is it, my brothers, if someone says he has faith but does not have works? Can that faith save him? If a brother or sister is poorly clothed and lacking in daily food, and one of you says to them, 'Go in peace, be warmed and filled,' without giving them the things needed for the body, what good is that? So also faith by itself, if it does not have works, is dead. (James 2:14-17)

> This is the message we have heard from him and proclaim to you, that God is light, and in him is no darkness at all. If we say we have fellowship with him while we walk in darkness, we lie and do not practice the truth. (1 John 1:5-6)

Each one of these passages describes someone who says all the right things but whose life shows they're not really saved. You can claim to be a Christian and not enter the kingdom of heaven. You can say you have faith but wind up with a dead faith that does not save. You can claim to have fellowship with God and wind up walking in the darkness. The point is clear: it's not enough to pay lip service to following Jesus.

In case we're misunderstood, our good works cannot save us. Fundamentally, a Christian is someone who has simply put their faith in Jesus (cf. Eph. 2:8, Gal. 2:16). A Christian is someone who has turned away from a life of rebellion against God in order to trust in Jesus' death and resurrection for salvation (cf. 1 Thess. 1:9). Jesus did everything necessary for His people's salvation; there's nothing left for us to do. We simply take hold of all that Christ has done for us through repentance and faith.

We must understand this, or else we'll lose everything. If we think our personal goodness makes us 'more' of a Christian—or that our lack of personal goodness makes us less of a Christian—then we're missing something. The only holiness worth anything is Jesus' holiness, and that's credited to us when we trust in Him.

Based on what we've said, it might seem like anyone who *says* they have faith in Jesus should be treated like a Christian. After all, it doesn't matter what they've done in the past or what they're doing now, right? God's love is always and only received as a free gift (Rom. 6:23). But there's another truth we have to hold together with our understanding of the freeness of salvation. It's this: whenever someone is saved by God's free grace, that grace transforms them. It produces certain changes in someone's life.

Okay, Then How Can We Know That Someone is Saved?

When I (Sean) was in the military, I was issued with some really cool gear. I needed this gear for various missions. As a pastor, I've sometimes wished that God gave us spiritual night-vision goggles, like the ones I used in the army. It would be so useful to have a tool that sees inside someone's heart to find out if they're truly a Christian. As cool as that would be, God in His wisdom hasn't given individuals or the church the ability to look inside someone's soul and see if they have a heart of stone or a heart of flesh (Ezek. 36:26). We can't know, finally, whether or not a professing Christian is truly converted.

But that doesn't mean we just throw our hands up and claim ignorance. We still have the responsibility to evaluate someone's profession of faith. For example, when professing believers fall into enduring patterns of unrepentant sin, the church is commanded to render a verdict on that person's claim to be a Christian. If you're unfamiliar with this, consider Paul's instructions to the church in 1 Corinthians 5:1-13. The same thing is true of professing believers and false doctrine; if professing believers come to believe in and confess a false gospel, then the church can and should be able to render a verdict on that believer's profession of faith (Gal. 1:8-9).

There are two things you are looking for when you are trying to evaluate someone's profession of faith: do they believe the truth, and do they live in light of it? Consider the words of the apostle John: 'Everyone who goes on ahead and does not abide in the teaching of Christ, does not have God. Whoever abides in the teaching has both the Father and the Son' (2 John 9).

The word *abide* is important. It speaks not only to the Christian's belief in the truth of the gospel, but also their ongoing commitment to living in light of those truths.

So here's the burning question: Is someone who believes the lies of the PG abiding in the teachings of Christ? It sure doesn't seem like it.

Think about it. Jesus says, 'Take up your cross and follow me.' The gospel says the cross is primarily about spiritual healing, but the prosperity gospel says that Jesus' atonement has purchased our health, wealth, and happiness. To believe the prosperity gospel is to believe a different message about Jesus and, in the process, to abandon the truth. Put simply, the apostle John says that to believe in any false gospel, including the prosperity gospel, is to not have God. (2 John 9)

Abiding in the teachings of Christ also means that we strive (imperfectly, to be sure) by the power of the Holy Spirit to put sin to death and to live in ways that are obedient and pleasing to the Lord. A Christian doesn't obey God *in order* to be accepted by Him, but rather *because* he has been accepted (Rom. 6:1-4). This is why the apostle John writes:

> No one who abides in him keeps on sinning; no one who keeps on sinning has either seen him or known him.

Little children, let no one deceive you. Whoever practices righteousness is righteous, as he is righteous. Whoever makes a practice of sinning is of the devil, for the devil has been sinning from the beginning. The reason the Son of God appeared was to destroy the works of the devil.' (1 John 3:6-8)

Let's make this practical. Imagine the following people:

- Jen is a professing Christian in your neighborhood. She's a member of a gospel-preaching, Bible-believing church in town. The church isn't perfect, but you know they worship Jesus and teach the Bible faithfully. Jen seems to be growing in her love for Christ, and she's striving to address areas in her life where she struggles with sin.

- Then there's Erica, a co-worker of yours. She professes Christ, too. She goes to church on a fairly regular basis. She posts a 'verse of the day' on her Instagram and refers to faith and God's blessings in almost every conversation. She has also mentioned to you on multiple occasions that she's living with her boyfriend of ten years. She knows it's 'not God's best' for her, but her boyfriend isn't all that interested in marriage and Erica isn't all that interested in being alone.

- Now consider Sam. He cuts your hair. He's a professing Christian who's a member of World Faith Center, a church down the road which has preached the PG for the past fifteen years. Sam says that he loves Jesus and wants to live faithfully as a Christian. But he also thinks that going to a doctor is sin. Moreover, Sam professes to be a 'little god' and to have the ability to speak healing into existence. One time, he overheard you talking about being broke and waiting for your next paycheck, and he told you that Christians should never confess poverty because God won't bless negative confessions.

How confident do you feel about these three people's professions of faith in the Lord Jesus? Jen says she trusts in Christ alone for her salvation, and her life seems consistent with that profession. Erica talks a good game, but she lives like her boyfriend is the most important thing in her life. Sam's life might seem OK on the surface, but his beliefs and motivations are out of whack.

In the end, Jen is the only one who should really have confidence that she belongs to the Lord. Erica may indeed be a Christian, and if she is, then the Lord will discipline her to remove that sin from her life (Heb. 12:7-11). Sam could be a believer, too, and if he is, the Holy Spirit will guide him into the truth eventually (John 16:13). But for the moment, their lives and beliefs make it impossible to affirm that they're really saved.

Nice, Not New

How is it possible that someone so kind, generous, and loving—someone who does so much 'for the Lord'—could be self-deceived and not actually a Christian?

Well, we should remember that the Bible has a category for people like this. In the Sermon on the Mount, Jesus devotes a pretty large chunk of time on what distinguishes a true disciple from a false one.

According to Jesus, we should expect to meet self-deceived people. So let's circle back and take another look at what Jesus says:

> Not everyone who says to me, 'Lord, Lord,' will enter the kingdom of heaven, but only the one who does the will of my Father who is in heaven. Many will say to me on that day, 'Lord, Lord, did we not prophesy in your name and in your name drive out demons and in your name perform many miracles?' Then I will tell them plainly, 'I never knew you. Away from me, you evildoers!' (Matt. 7:21-23, NIV)

You'll notice that these people—Jesus calls them 'evildoers,' by the way—do all kinds of impressive things in the name of Jesus. He then makes the terrifying claim that these same people will try to get into heaven by highlighting all of the really cool and kind 'ministry stuff' they did here on earth. But that won't be enough. It won't matter. Jesus will plainly tell them 'I don't know you.' Pastors, Sunday school teachers, missionaries, traveling evangelists, faith healers, nuns, and nursery workers. It doesn't matter. The point is clear: doing things *for* Jesus is not the same thing as belonging *to* Jesus.

Jesus then tells us how to spot a false teacher:

> You will recognize them by their fruits. Are grapes gathered from thornbushes, or figs from thistles? So, every healthy tree bears good fruit, but the diseased tree bears bad fruit. A healthy tree cannot bear bad fruit, nor can a diseased tree bear good fruit. Every tree that does not bear good fruit is cut down and thrown into the fire. Thus you will recognize them by their fruits.' (Matt. 7:16-20)

It's quite possible to be heavily involved in 'ministry' without actually knowing God. As a matter of fact, the more ministry false professors do, the more surprised they'll be when they find themselves cut down and thrown into the fire.

One final matter to consider from this text. Jesus seems to imply that most of these false prophets and fake disciples won't find out that they've been deceived until it's too late. Many kind and hard-working people doing good, seemingly Christian stuff won't know they're self-deceived until they stand before the throne of Christ.

We need to understand what Jesus means when He says Christians 'bear fruit.' Christians should pray and read their Bibles. But the Bible never refers to these activities as 'fruit.' As a matter of fact, in the Sermon on the Mount, Jesus calls attention to the fact that the Pharisees pray (Matt. 6:5-15), fast (Matt. 6:16-18), and give to the poor (Matt. 6:1-4). And yet, it's all rotten fruit because it's done with the wrong attitude! According to Jesus, it's possible to do *good* things in a way that bears *bad* fruit. As one pastor friend has put it, Jesus didn't come to make us nice, but to make us new.[1]

When we ask whether or not someone is a follower of Christ, we're asking if they've been made new, whether they've been born again by God's Spirit (John 3:3). That new birth happens on the inside; it's not like a tattoo or a haircut that we can see immediately. Instead, it manifests itself in genuine faith in Christ and a new relationship to sin.

---

1   Michael Lawrence, *Conversion* (Wheaton, IL: Crossway, 2017).

So, do TBN viewers go to heaven? It's certainly possible. In fact, we're confident in saying that many probably do. Remember, we're saved by grace alone through faith alone in Christ alone. It's possible that true sheep have been warped by false doctrine, but they are still fundamentally trusting in Christ. People sometimes believe inconsistent things. So maybe someone is really trusting in Christ as Lord and Savior, even though they have wrong views of their ability to 'claim blessing' or 'bind the devil' or 'believe God's promise to heal right now.'

That said, if a TBN watcher *or anyone on the planet* loves stuff or health or marriage or their own lives more than God, then, no, they don't truly know God, and they will not be saved. If God is not a person's deepest desire, but He's just a means to another end, to their true object of worship, whether it's health, wealth, or a sense of personal worth, then, no, they don't know God. God is not their god. That other thing is their god. Anyone who truly knows God knows He's better than life itself (Matt. 16:24-26).[2]

Rather than asking if a certain individual who buys into the PG is really a Christian, we should ask, 'Can we have confidence in their profession of faith?' We are confident in Christ's power to save the worst of sinners, and in the end we can't have confidence that anyone who persists in believing a false gospel is a true disciple of Jesus.

---

2   For more on this idea, check out Mike's book *Am I Really a Christian?* No, seriously, check it out. He has kids in college, and every bit helps.

6. Should We Pray Together?

After the last chapter, you might feel a tension between several important biblical principles. On one hand, believers in Christ are instructed to treat one another with kindness, charity, and mercy (e.g., Rom. 12:10). We should bear patiently with our brothers and sisters and maintain unity with them (e.g., Eph. 4:1-6), even if we disagree with them on certain issues.

On the other hand, we're also instructed not to tolerate certain doctrines, behaviors, and false gospels in the church (e.g., Rev. 2:14-16).

So how do we relate to our friends and family members who claim to believe the true gospel but have been deceived by the PG? How should we think about and relate to those teachers and their ministries?

Sheep, Goats, and Wolves

Scripture gives us all sorts of images that help us understand a believer's relationship with Jesus.

- He is the head; we are the body (Col. 1:18).
- He is the king; we are His citizens (John 18:36).
- He is the master; we are the bondservants (John 15:20). But one of Jesus' favorite word pictures is that of a shepherd and his sheep (e.g., Matt. 10:6, 15:24, and 26:31).
- Jesus is the shepherd; we are His sheep (1 Pet. 2:25). This powerful image highlights the tender care of Jesus as He relates to us.

But in Matthew 25, this word picture takes a darker twist. Jesus speaks of a future day when He will come in glory and separate people from each other 'as a shepherd separates the sheep from the goats' (v. 32). The sheep are true followers of Jesus; they will ultimately be welcomed to 'inherit the kingdom' (v. 34). The goats, however, represent people who are opposed to Jesus; they will ultimately be ushered into 'the eternal fire prepared for the devil and his angels' (v 41).

While we're talking about wildlife, let's throw one more critter into the mix: wolves. They want to devour Jesus' flock. Sometimes, these wolves are outside the church, like when Jesus talks about sending His disciples out as 'lambs in the midst of wolves' (Luke 10:3). But 'wolves' can also arise from within the church, like when Jesus says, 'Beware of false prophets, who come to you in sheep's clothing but inwardly are ravenous wolves' (Matt. 7:15).

Some wolves disguise themselves as sheep so that the flock won't see them coming. Jesus wants us to have a category for 'sheep' that aren't really sheep but are dangerous predators.

'Beware,' He says, because if you let a wolf get too close the consequences for your soul can be disastrous.

How Do We Spot a Wolf?

No pastor, preacher, leader, or teacher has an utterly perfect understanding of the Bible. Every one of us is beset by some combination of misunderstanding, folly, and failure. But a pastor isn't a wolf just because he holds to a few theologically incorrect positions. If that were true, then Baptists like us would have to say our Presbyterian brothers were wolves— and vice versa.

Rather, a wolf ravages the flock of God, trying to draw disciples away from the true gospel of Christ. Look at the way the apostle Paul describes wolves when he warns the elders of the Ephesian church: 'I know that after my departure fierce wolves will come in among you, not sparing the flock; and from among your own selves will arise men speaking twisted things, to draw away the disciples after them' (Acts 20:29-30). Wolves are a threat to the gospel of God and the Church of God.

Since Jesus is 'the way, the truth, and the life' and no one can approach the Father but through Him (John 14:6), it makes sense that Satan would send out men who preach lies in Jesus' name.

So, how do we identify a wolf? Fortunately, the authors of the New Testament helped believers do just that. Here's what they tell us:

Wolves deceive and distort. According to the apostle Peter, false prophets among the flock will bring in all sorts of heresies (2 Pet. 2:1), even to the point of denying the Lord

Jesus Himself. Jude tells his readers that wicked teachers in the church will rely on their dreams rather than teaching people the Bible (Jude 8). False teachers say blasphemous things (Jude 8-10, 2 Pet. 2:12), denigrating God's glory and exalting themselves. They twist the Word of God to make it say things it doesn't really say (2 Pet. 3:16), and they distort the gospel into a message that cannot save anyone (Gal. 1:6-7).

So, if someone teaches that Jesus isn't fully God and fully man (2 John 7), or if he teaches that we can become mini-gods, or if he teaches that we can be perfectly holy and healthy in this life, or that Jesus is Satan's half-brother—well, then you can be sure that person is a wolf.

Wolves devour and destroy. The Bible's image of a wolf among sheep is fitting because it calls to mind a ravenous predator chasing down his prey to satisfy his appetite. And that's exactly what many wolves do to the flock of God. They're not motivated by a desire to help people worship Christ or grow in holiness. Instead, they want to make themselves rich off the gifts of deceived church members (see 1 Tim. 6:5 and Titus 1:11). Many wolves are also motivated by their sexual lusts; they see the flock of God as a hunting ground where they can satisfy their perverted desires. Any modern-day story of a pastor who leads a member of his church into sexual sin has an ancient pedigree (2 Pet. 2:14, Jude 4, Rev. 2:20).

So, if you see a pastor of an impoverished church driving a BMW that his congregation bought for him, or a leader who is inappropriate with members of the opposite sex (or, the same sex), or someone whose teaching promotes greed and selfishness, then you can be sure that person is a wolf.

It's also worth mentioning that wolves often have some sort of authority or platform. They could be a pastor, a missionary, or a traveling evangelist. Whether or not they have an official position, they wield influence. Wolves can influence the church with false doctrine. Your Aunt Janice may believe some weird stuff about healing, but it's unlikely she'll lead others to hell from her La-Z-Boy where she sits watching Benny Hinn with the volume turned way up. But the pastor of a church, the president of a seminary, a missionary on the field, a pink-haired prophetess on TBN, or an author who can sell 1,000 books a month—that person is positioned to do some real damage to the sheep.

How Should We Treat a Wolf?

It seems like it has become sadly common for otherwise faithful pastors, teachers, and authors to share ministry platforms with those who preach a gospel different than the gospel that was once for all delivered to the saints (Jude 3). These ministers lend their hard-won credibility to a man or woman whose goal—intentionally or not—is to devour and deceive Christ's sheep.

Fortunately, we don't have to guess what we should do with wolves. The much-neglected little book of 2 John speaks directly to the issue. John's message is not complicated: Christians must strive for gospel harmony in matters of love, truth, and obedience as they follow Jesus. Those who love God and one another will walk in obedience and love the truth (v. 4, 6).

John wrote the letter because false teachers were trying to lead the Church into a kind of Christianity that prized obedience and love, but not truth. Specifically, it seems like these teachers lied about Jesus (v. 7), so the Spirit prompted John to put pen to parchment and warn his beloved children that their souls were in danger (v. 8). After showing the great danger that these false teachers represented to the flock and warning them not to fall victim to their deceit, the apostle makes a very clear point of application: 'If anyone comes to you and does not bring this teaching, do not receive him into your house or give him any greeting, for whoever greets him takes part in his wicked works' (2 John 10-11).

John warns against any kind of action that would lead the watching world to believe that we, as ambassadors of Christ and torchbearers of the true gospel, are on the same team as these deceivers. A true follower of Christ doesn't have the same boss as a wolf. We're not part of the same family. We don't worship the same God, and we don't preach the same gospel.

Our actions shouldn't leave any room for confusion. The distinction between true shepherds and wolves must be crystal clear. When churches, missions agencies, parachurch ministries, and other Christian organizations receive false teachers as they would receive a true minister of the gospel, they give the false impression that deceivers aren't that dangerous after all. This blasé approach to gospel partnership will result in precious sheep being exposed to eternal danger because the very people entrusted by Christ to care for them thought it would be okay.

John's warning is stark: if pastors or ministers of the gospel of any kind receive or greet these kinds of false teachers, they are essentially participating in their wickedness (v. 11).

Church members and pastors must not, in any way or under any circumstance, lock arms with heretical teachers, pastors, authors, professors, or *anyone in any capacity* who preaches a different gospel message.

Let's be specific. Followers of Christ shouldn't participate with anyone who claims to be a Christian but who proclaims a false gospel in:

- Ministry conferences
- Prayer breakfasts
- Co-leading Bible studies
- Pastors' coalitions, networks, or associations
- Evangelistic parachurch ministries
- Pulpit swaps
- Recommending their books, sharing their articles, promoting their websites

Some situations might be different. It requires wisdom to know when to draw the line. We're not recommending an arbitrary form of separationism. We simply believe Scripture teaches that we must not align ourselves with false teachers or any of their ministries in ways that will lead to confusion about the gospel.

We realize that adapting this approach might lead people to view you as mean-spirited, divisive, unloving, and unconcerned with the unity of the Church. It would certainly make you unpopular in some circles. Let it be so. We must walk in the way of love, which is inextricably connected to truth. We must protect the flock. We must confess the true Jesus. We must not partake in wickedness. We must abide in the truth of our master.

In the end, we want to be precisely as divisive as the Holy Spirit who inspired 2 John encourages us to be, and that means we must divide from all people who lie about Jesus and desire to devour His sheep.

'But I Thought We Weren't Supposed to Judge'

This is quite easy to say, but difficult to do. After all, we don't like judgmental and self-righteous people. Some will even point to the Bible and say Jesus told us to 'judge not' (Matt. 7:1). Shouldn't we believe the best about people and give them the benefit of the doubt? If they claim to love Jesus, shouldn't that be enough? Besides, why is it any of our business?

But Christians are told to render judgment on these kinds of things. Jesus calls His Church to carry out judgment in His name and under His authority (Matt. 18:15-20, 1 Cor. 5:1-13). In Matthew 7:1, Jesus prohibits self-righteous, hypocritical judgment. Elsewhere in Scripture, we're told to judge the differences between the true gospel and true gospel professors.

Christians are repeatedly told to be on guard against false teachers (see Matt. 24:24, Acts 20:31, and 1 John 4:1-6). Church leaders in particular are called to protect the flock from wolves (Acts 20:28, Titus 1:9), and individual churches will be held responsible if they listen to or tolerate a false teacher (Rev. 2:14, 20). This is why Paul told the churches in Galatia that they were obligated not to listen to anyone who preached a false gospel:

> But even if we or an angel from heaven should preach to you a gospel contrary to the one we preached to you, let him be accursed. As we have said before, so now I say again: If anyone is preaching to you a gospel contrary to the one you received, let him be accursed. (Gal. 1:8-9)

Jude had a similar message:

> Beloved, although I was very eager to write to you about our common salvation, I found it necessary to write appealing to you to contend for the faith that was once for all delivered to the saints. For certain people have crept in unnoticed who long ago were designated for this condemnation, ungodly people, who pervert the grace of our God into sensuality and deny our only Master and Lord, Jesus Christ. (Jude 3-4)

These instructions require Christians—both individually and corporately—to render judgments on the teaching they hear.

In the end, it doesn't matter much whether or not a teacher has good intentions. We might like to think that the preacher on TV has a good heart full of good motives, but good intentions don't turn a lie into the truth. We cannot see into a man's heart, and we can only hazard a guess as to why they do and say the things that they do. Our job is to evaluate the message they proclaim in light of the truth of the gospel.

If someone broke into your home, you wouldn't spend a ton of time giving them the benefit of the doubt or trying to discern their motives. You wouldn't wait to find out if he was a good guy who just happened to be down on his luck, or a bad guy who enjoyed doing harm. The intentions of the heart don't really matter when there's a serious threat.

The same thing is true regarding false teachers. In 2 John, the Apostle commands his readers to do two things:

1. Watch out for their own souls (v. 8)
2. Evaluate the teaching of those who preach the gospel (v. 10)

John doesn't encourage Christians to get to know a false teacher. He doesn't tell them to build a relationship and develop rapport with him. Why? Because souls are at stake! God's Word couldn't be any clearer: 'Everyone who goes on ahead and does not abide in the teaching of Christ, does not have God' (2 John 9a). To lead God's people away from Jesus by preaching a different gospel is wicked (v. 11); the preacher's intentions are beside the point.

What About Deceived Sheep?

Now it might be helpful to think about the sheep. As every pastor knows, there are weak sheep, strong sheep, immature sheep, proud sheep, injured sheep, uninformed sheep, confused sheep, and even goats who think they're sheep but aren't. Many of those who believe in some form of the prosperity gospel are true sheep who genuinely don't know better. They're confused, immature, weak, hungry, and often hurting. It's important that we don't treat these sheep like goats or wolves.

Christians often ask us how to interact with family members, friends, and co-workers who believe the prosperity gospel. They understand that Scripture teaches us not to lock arms with false teachers, but they aren't so sure what to do about their 'crazy uncle' who wants to plead the healing power of the blood of Jesus over their neighbor during a prayer walk, or their mother who refuses to acknowledge sickness because she thinks that doing so is an admission of doubt. Can we pray with our 'crazy uncle'? Should we go to church with our mom when we know she goes to a prosperity gospel church?

It's important to remember that our theology doesn't exist in a vacuum. What we believe about the gospel, and about those who profess to believe the gospel, has real consequences for our lives. The gospel can—and often does—cause real rifts in close relationships. Jesus knows this (Matt. 10:34-37). We have to be open to the possibility that, despite our attempts to communicate with love and grace, our insistence on the true gospel may offend and alienate people we love. If that's the case, so be it.

But that's certainly not always the case. Few answers will apply in every situation; it takes wisdom to know when to speak and when to exercise patience. In the end, the most important question is whether or not the person in question has repented of their sins and trusted in Jesus for their salvation . If so, then we can be sure that the love of God abides with that person and the Holy Spirit will bring them to greater conformity to Christ.

In the end, we want to see people as Jesus sees. The Lord is very patient and loving and merciful with His sheep. He condemns those wolves who would hurt His flock. That's a pretty good guide for how we ought to relate to those two groups of people.

7. The Prosperity Gospel Among the Orthodox

As we begin the final chapter, we want to suggest one more important fact: it's possible to believe in the prosperity gospel and not even be aware of it. More specifically, we might reject the PG as a set of doctrines, yet unwittingly embrace it in how we live and relate to God. We may reject this constellation of false teachings *in theory* but actually adhere to them *in practice*.

After all, the prosperity gospel wears different masks, and those masks typically look like us. It promises whatever people in a nation, age, economic group, political ideology, or tribe most want. If you're an African dirt farmer, it promises goats that give milk and chickens that lay eggs. If you're an upper-middle-class American, it promises a purpose-filled life, successful marriages, and happy adult children.

In other words, if someone says the words 'prosperity gospel church' and you picture in your mind's eye a group of people culturally, nationally, economically, or ethnically different than your own, you might have missed how the prosperity gospel targets you.

So, how can we know that we ourselves are being led astray by the prosperity gospel? In short, we should look at our actions.

Sadly, our actions sometimes show that deep down in our heart of hearts we don't *really* believe everything we claim to believe. We know what we *should* believe, but those things don't actually filter down into our hearts and ultimately into our actions.

If you've ever been hesitant to get on a ride at an amusement park, you may have experienced something of what we're talking about here. Your brain has plenty of reasons to believe that you will be safe while hurtling around in the air: the ride has operated safely up to this point, it's been planned out by engineers in accordance with the laws of physics, and the amusement park has an economic interest in their rides being completely safe. And yet, you may still be reluctant to risk your health and safety. You believe that it's safe, but your actions show that you *really* aren't sure.

When it comes to theology and doctrine, we can be tempted to be satisfied with affirming the truth of the Bible. And while that's certainly important, it's not everything. For this reason, James reminds us: 'But be doers of the word, and not hearers only, deceiving yourselves' (James 1:22). And as Paul reminds Timothy, it's important to keep a careful watch over both your doctrine *and* your life (1 Timothy 4:16). It's good to be a thinker and a hearer of the truth, but we need to live the truth out.

Now, you might not try to speak things into existence. You might never give money expecting to get a massive payday in return. You may not expect God to heal your every disease. But we should not let ourselves off the hook so easily.

In Luke 18, we read about Jesus' interaction with a man who wanted to know what it meant to be a disciple:

And a ruler asked him, 'Good Teacher, what must I do to inherit eternal life?' And Jesus said to him, 'Why do you call me good? No one is good except God alone. You know the commandments: "Do not commit adultery, Do not murder, Do not steal, Do not bear false witness, Honor your father and mother."' And he said, 'All these I have kept from my youth.' When Jesus heard this, he said to him, 'One thing you still lack. Sell all that you have and distribute to the poor, and you will have treasure in heaven; and come, follow me.' But when he heard these things, he became very sad, for he was extremely rich. Jesus, seeing that he had become sad, said, 'How difficult it is for those who have wealth to enter the kingdom of God! For it is easier for a camel to go through the eye of a needle than for a rich person to enter the kingdom of God.' Those who heard it said, 'Then who can be saved?' But he said, 'What is impossible with man is possible with God.' And Peter said, 'See, we have left our homes and followed you.' And he said to them, 'Truly, I say to you, there is no one who has left house or wife or brothers or parents or children, for the sake of the kingdom of God, who will not receive many times more in this time, and in the age to come eternal life.' (Luke 18:18-30)

Maybe you can identify with the rich ruler here. You know what it feels like to be excited and willing to do whatever Jesus says—just tell me how high and I'll jump! This young man had shown he was willing to do whatever was needed to inherit eternal life, including keeping all of the Law as he understood it. But when Jesus showed him the level of commitment that would be required of him, he walked away from eternal life.

Now, don't misunderstand what's happening in this interaction. Jesus isn't saying that everyone needs to sell everything they have in order to follow Him. Instead, Jesus has put His finger on the one thing in his life that this rich ruler thinks he cannot live without. He idolized his extreme wealth, and when faced with the choice between his money and Jesus' gift of eternal life, he simply walked away. When you have a lot of money, it's much harder to leave everything and follow Jesus (harder than a camel going through the eye of a needle, Jesus says).

You probably see how this connects to our discussion of the PG. Jesus says that following Him means giving away what we might normally treasure most. And while we may not embrace the excesses of the 'name it and claim it' crowd, that's not enough. We need to ask ourselves whether we hold everything in our lives with an open hand, ready for God to take it or re-deploy it for His good pleasure. If not, we may have subtly embraced the PG's notions of what it means to be blessed by God. If we're only willing to follow Jesus if we can have what we would want anyway, then we're disciples of the PG, not Jesus Christ.

So ask yourself: is there something Jesus could ask you to give up that you wouldn't be willing to let go, no matter what?

Let's brainstorm how this might look in our lives. What if Jesus asked you:

- To cut your salary in half in order to take a job that would serve His Church more effectively?
- To move elsewhere so that you might spread the gospel (see Heb. 11:8)?
- To give away a big chunk of your retirement savings because He knows that security is an idol for you?
- To sacrifice some of your peace and convenience to serve and love your neighbors?
- To leave your normal social circles in order to befriend people from another culture living in your town?
- To open your home to a recovering addict even if there's a possibility he might take advantage of you?
- To lend your second car to a missionary family who has come home on furlough?
- To give more of your time to your local church and be actively involved in loving that body?
- To show the glory of the gospel by adopting an orphan?
- To stand up for a particular person or issue, even if doing so will cost you your job?
- To be mocked and ridiculed as backwards and bigoted for following Jesus?

The author of Hebrews spends most of his message talking to his readers about how they're suffering because they're following Christ. But he's also quick to remind them that things could be worse—much worse. They could be like the saints of old who 'suffered mocking and flogging, and even chains and imprisonment. They were stoned, they were sawn in two, they were killed with the sword. They went about in skins of sheep and goats, destitute, afflicted, mistreated' (Heb. 11:36-37).

This call to suffer shouldn't come as a surprise. After all, Jesus Himself was put to death on a Roman cross, and most of the twelve disciples suffered a violent death. Since then, millions of God's children have given their lives for the name of Jesus.

- Some Christians were thrown to the wild beasts.
- Others were beaten and stoned to death like Stephen (Acts 7:54-60).
- Polycarp, William Tyndale, and Jan Huss were burned at the stake.
- Jim Elliot and his fellow missionaries died at the tip of the spear.
- An untold number of saints have given their lives trying to take the gospel of Jesus Christ to the ends of the earth, from missionaries in North Korea to house church pastors in China to evangelists in the hills of Pakistan.

We can't tell you exactly what following Jesus will cost you in terms of time, talent, treasure, safety, security, control, good looks, reputation, physical health, emotional health, personal preference, independence, and autonomy. But we can tell you that He calls all of us to die to something.

When we balk at that call, we're functionally living out the principles of the PG.

Looking Into Your Heart

The goal in this chapter is to encourage introspection, to see what things might be trying to dethrone Jesus in your heart. So ask yourself: what makes you really anxious? What do you love so much that the thought of losing it makes you feel panicky?

In the Sermon on the Mount, Jesus addresses a crowd. Many of them were poor; they had no clue where tomorrow's bread would come from. Maybe you identify with what that feels like. Here's what Jesus tells them:

> Therefore I tell you, do not be anxious about your life, what you will eat or what you will drink, nor about your body, what you will put on. Is not life more than food, and the body more than clothing? Look at the birds of the air: they neither sow nor reap nor gather into barns, and yet your heavenly Father feeds them. Are you not of more value than they? And which of you by being anxious can add a single hour to his span of life? And why are you anxious about clothing? Consider the lilies of the field, how they grow: they neither toil nor spin, yet I tell you, even Solomon in all his glory was not arrayed like one of these. But if God so clothes the grass of the field, which today is alive and tomorrow is thrown into the oven, will he not much more clothe you, O you of little faith? Therefore do not be anxious, saying, 'What shall we eat?' or 'What shall we drink?' or 'What shall we wear?' For the Gentiles seek after all these things, and your heavenly Father knows that you need them all. But

seek first the kingdom of God and his righteousness, and all these things will be added to you. (Matt. 6:25-33)

You see what Jesus is doing, don't you? He's lifting the eyes of His hearers off their material possessions—or their lack of material possessions—and refocusing them on their heavenly Father. Jesus says that Gentiles (by which He means 'unbelievers') invest their time and energy in worrying about such things. But those who have God as their Father through faith in Jesus are freed from such anxieties. Instead, they 'seek first the kingdom of God and his righteousness.' Simply put, our anxieties often reveal what we care about most.

Here's another set of questions to ask yourself:

- What am I working for?
- What am I trying to achieve with my life and my time?
- What kind of reward am I working for?

In the same sermon, Jesus begins to address those with plenty in reserve. Maybe that fits your situation a bit more closely. Here's what He says:

Do not lay up for yourselves treasures on earth, where moth and rust destroy and where thieves break in and steal, but lay up for yourselves treasures in heaven, where neither moth nor rust destroys and where thieves do not break in and steal. For where your treasure is, there your heart will be also.... No one can serve two masters, for either he will hate the one and love the other, or he will be devoted to the one and despise the other. You cannot serve God and money. (Matt. 6:19-21, 24)

Most people are working for something, whether it's a nice vacation, the ability to stay ahead of the bills each month, a new car, or even retirement. But here Jesus warns us against laying up treasure on earth. Our money and houses and fancy clothes can disappear in a moment—an earthquake, a fire, or a thief can make short work of them all. And even if you get through life unscathed, you can be sure that the grave will take them away. For this reason, Jesus urges the well-off to invest their money and their energy in something that pays eternal, everlasting dividends. He tells them to lay up for themselves treasure in heaven. He encourages them to be generous, benevolent, and kind with their riches.

Both a rich man and a poor man can be enslaved to money, if riches are what they care about most in the world. Likewise, both a rich man and a poor man can store up treasures in heaven, if they prize God above all else. The important question is not how much money you have, but who gets to determine what you do with it. If Jesus is the true north on your compass, then the decisions you make will tend to store up treasure in heaven. But if you want the things of earth more than anything else, then that's all you'll get.

Jesus puts a fine point on it: what you do with your money and your life reveals who you serve. If you love money and live for storing up treasure in the here and now, money will be your master. But if you love God and live for what He says is valuable, then He will be your master.

Now *that's* the most important question: who is your master? In whom have you placed your hope and trust?

Yourself? The watered-down genie-in-a-bottle Jesus of the PG? Or the real Jesus of the Bible, who suffered for us and calls us to follow Him to the cross? Whose opinion controls what you prioritize? What matters to you most, and what could you never imagine having to part with? Do you love Jesus and His people most, or when it boils down to it, do you really love yourself as you should?

Jesus is not a half-way Savior. He's either Lord over our entire lives, or He's not Lord of our lives at all. As is commonly observed, there's not a single square inch of the universe which Jesus doesn't claim as His own, which means there's not a single square inch of your life that Jesus will allow you to keep for yourself. In a twisted way, the PG inverts this relationship. In the PG, God becomes a servant of our desires, and we become the ones whose will should be done.

And so perhaps the best way to keep the arms and tentacles of the PG from wrapping themselves around our hearts is to continually remind ourselves of the goodness and beauty and strength of our God. He alone has the power and wisdom and authority to determine the course of our lives. And He alone has the love and goodness and kindness that deserve our allegiance.

Remember Psalm 73? We talked about it earlier. A man named Asaph wrote it perhaps in the darkest hour of his life. And it's in this moment of great suffering that he's able to have an unobstructed view of where his true love and affection lies. So much so, that he writes these words: **'Whom have I in heaven but you? And there is nothing**

on earth that I desire besides you. My flesh and my heart may fail, but God is the strength of my heart and my portion forever' (Ps. 73:25-26).

In the end, the PG fails because it can't teach us to pray these words because these words can only come from the lips of people who have set their hearts on the Lord as their greatest treasure. May we all pray these words until we finally see our God face-to-face.

9Marks

Building Healthy Churches

9Marks exists to equip church leaders with a biblical vision and practical resources for displaying God's glory to the nations through healthy churches.

To that end, we want to see churches characterized by these nine marks of health:

1   Expositional Preaching
2   Biblical Theology
3   A Biblical Understanding of the Gospel
4   A Biblical Understanding of Conversion
5   A Biblical Understanding of Evangelism
6   Biblical Church Membership
7   Biblical Church Discipline
8   Biblical Discipleship
9   Biblical Church Leadership

Find more titles at
www.9Marks.org

Also Available from Christian Focus Publications…

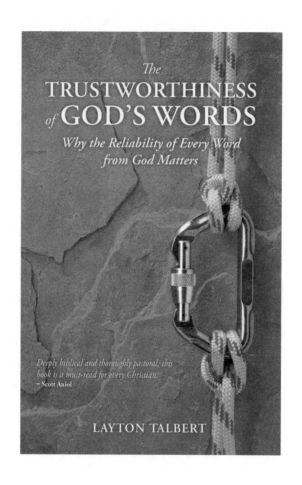

The
TRUSTWORTHINESS
of GOD'S WORDS
*Why the Reliability of Every Word
from God Matters*

*Deeply biblical and thoroughly pastoral, this
book is a must-read for every Christian.*
– Scott Aniol

LAYTON TALBERT

ISBN 978-1-5271-0790-8

The Trustworthiness of God's Words

Why the Reliability of Every Word from God Matters

Layton Talbert

This is a book about God's jealousy for His integrity, His passion to be believed, on the basis of His words alone. Throughout Scripture God expresses His determination to be known as the God who keeps His words. He has resolved that every person and nation will see and confess that all His words are reliable down to every last syllable, jot, and tittle. Learning to trust a God who is sovereign and in control, especially in the ache and throb of life, means hanging on to the conviction that everything He says is utterly dependable.

… he meticulously shows from Scripture itself that God is true to his word, and that great blessings and comfort come to those who trust him. Deeply biblical and thoroughly pastoral, this book is a must–read for every Christian.

Scott Aniol

Executive Vice President and Editor–in–Chief of G3 Ministries

Hermeneutically nuanced. Theologically sound. Pastorally sensitive. Layton Talbert offers both the church and the academy a valuable service here. I heartily recommend it to God's people as an antidote to unbelief in God's Word.

A. Philip Brown II

Professor of Bible and Theology, Graduate Program Director, God's Bible School and College (Cincinnati, Ohio)

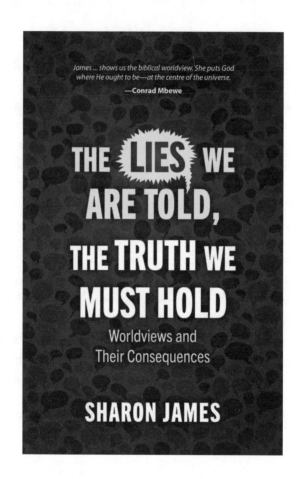

James ... shows us the biblical worldview. She puts God where He ought to be—at the centre of the universe.

—**Conrad Mbewe**

THE LIES WE ARE TOLD, THE TRUTH WE MUST HOLD

Worldviews and Their Consequences

SHARON JAMES

ISBN 978-1-5271-0796-0

The Lies We Are Told, The Truth We Must Hold

Worldviews and Their Consequences

We are surrounded by lies. They are incorporated into the worldview of our culture. We daily absorb them, and these lies can have deadly effects on individuals, societies and whole civilisations.

Sharon James investigates the origins of some of these lies and looks at how we have got to the point where 'my truth' is as valid as 'your truth', and absolute truth is an outdated way of thinking. In examining the evidence of history, she highlights the consequences of applying dangerous untruths. She also looks at how Christians often respond to the culture's lies – in silence, acquiescence or celebration of them – and why these responses can be as harmful as the lies themselves.

This book aims to equip Christians to navigate the minefield of current claims. To understand our inherent human significance, to know genuine freedom, and to work for real justice, we need to know the truth.

… a remarkable feat: she addresses the lies that our culture currently exalts as truth and does so in a way that crosses the generational divide and will be helpful both to young people and those who wish to understand them and help them think through the deepest challenges of our day.

Carl R. Trueman

Professor of Biblical and Religious Studies, Grove City College, Pennsylvania

Christian Focus Publications

Our mission statement —

STAYING FAITHFUL

In dependence upon God we seek to impact the world
through literature faithful to His infallible Word, the Bible.
Our aim is to ensure that the Lord Jesus Christ is presented as
the only hope to obtain forgiveness of sin, live a useful life and
look forward to heaven with Him.

Our books are published in four imprints:

CHRISTIAN
FOCUS

Popular works including biographies, commentaries, basic doctrine
and Christian living.

CHRISTIAN
HERITAGE

Books representing some of the
best material from the rich heritage
of the church.

MENTOR

Books written at a level suitable
for Bible College and seminary
students, pastors, and other serious readers. The imprint includes
commentaries, doctrinal studies,
examination of current issues and
church history.

CF4•K

Children's books for reading and
teaching and for all age groups, Sunday
school curriculum, puzzle and activity
books; personal and family devotional
titles, biographies and inspirational stories — because you are never too young
to know Jesus!

Christian Focus Publications Ltd,
Geanies House, Fearn, Ross-shire,
IV20 1TW, Scotland, United Kingdom.
www.christianfocus.com